D0427270

TRAILER GIRL

and other stories

Also by Terese Svoboda

FICTION

Cannibal

A Drink Called Paradise

POETRY

Mere Mortals

Laughing Africa

All Aberration

TRANSLATION

Cleaned the Crocodile's Teeth

TRAILER GIRL

and other stories

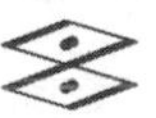

Terese Svoboda

COUNTERPOINT
WASHINGTON, D.C.

"Sundress" in *Manoa*, reprinted in *Sudden Fiction (Continued)*, Norton. "Electricity," "Water," and "What Did You Bring Me?" in *Columbia.* "I Dreamt He Fell Three Floors and Lived" and "Doll" in *Quarterly.* "Polio" in *Many Lights in Many Windows*, Milkweed Editions. "Psychic" in *Barnabe Review.* "Leadership" in *Bomb*, reprinted in *The Beacon Best of 1999: Creative Writing by Women and Men of All Colors*, Beacon Press. "Party Girl" and "A Mamma" in *Mississippi Review.* "Car Frogs" in *Lit.* "White" in *Conjunctions. Trailer Girl* excerpted in *Poetry Calendar.*

My most sincere thanks for those who helped me think about this book: Amy Hempel, Sheila Kohler, Molly Giles, Sondra Olsen, Gay Walley, William Melvin Kelley, Fran Gordon, Linda Hartinian, and my dear Steve Bull.

LIBRARY OF CONGRESS CATALOGING-IN-PUBLICATION DATA
Svoboda, Terese.
Trailer girl & other stories / by Terese Svoboda.
p. cm.
ISBN 1-58243-085-3
I. Title: Trailer girl and other stoires. II. Title.
PS3569.V6 T7 2001
813'.54—dc21 00-064447

FIRST PRINTING

Jacket and text design by Amy Evans McClure

COUNTERPOINT
P.O. Box 65793
Washington, D.C. 20035-5793

Counterpoint is a member of the Perseus Books Group

10 9 8 7 6 5 4 3 2 1

To My Beloved Sisters:

Amy, Kate, Jane, and Mary

Contents

. . . she seeks to find again
the dead child within herself,
even to revive it.

SIMONE DE BEAUVOIR

TRAILER GIRL

1

I TALK LIKE A LADY WHO KNOWS what she wants, and other things which I would mention but Ernie's charging over here with kids behind, screaming like they are chasing him and not vice versa and him whipping a cut aerial like a wild man.

I get the tea instead.

My hands hold the tea and a can and an opener as I make my way backward, rear first, out the front end and down the cinderblock pile that is my stair. I heap it all onto my card table and yell, What's the story?

Ernie is huffing and puffing all the way down my trailer-side and the aerial is bowing for or against me. I duck.

Those kids, he says, and almost gets one.

But they disappear. There's no thin air around here, but kids have a way with the edges of things. By the time Ernie's huffed and puffed his buttoned-down self across the four corners of my frontage, they've high-tailed it, they've gone.

See this? They broke it off, clean off the front. It's not that the truck was ever going to win any fancy costume contest or even turn over again, but to take the aerial——

Tea? I ask, being that the water I got going on the card table is boiling away and I do want a drop before it's gone.

No, thank you, he says. Then he says, Why don't you get the fence barb clean, that's what you're here for. But not nasty, no, just in a kind of drone that he goes into when being the guy-in-charge comes over him and he has to say something, especially when his first something doesn't mount up the way it should, given his position, and the kids and theirs, and the aerial now down.

I think out my answer so I don't snap back at his back-handed harping. I will clean the fence on Tuesday, I say, and I put my already-used-three-times tea bag into my cup and pour the hot water all over it, missing with some, drenching the dirt, why I keep my table outside in the first place. Is Tuesday okay?

Tuesday is soon I guess, he says, and he walks right up to the fence and pokes at the barb with the aerial. Nothing of the stuff stuck to it comes off but he keeps on poking.

I open my can a turn and four cats show. Want some? I

say to Ernie instead of to the cats or me, which is who this is for, a nice hot catfood lunch in a pot on a hotplate.

Ernie sees the tossed can and his nose wrinkles his whole face. Instead of saying, he produces what? from his back pants pocket, from under that buttoned flap men sometimes get there, he produces a wad all stapled together of tickets. Tuesday is when these are due, he says, and he flattens the wad on my table, smiles up at me with my tea in front of my catfood cooking. How about a chance?

I sip. Behind me tacked to the jigged-open front flap of a door hang plenty of chances, some for girl scouts, some for jamborees, some just chances taken like a turn at the slot machine—for anybody or thing.

I shoo the cat that's pawing the pot. Do I have to be present?

They say no but it never hurts. It's only in town, for the clinic in town. You know these places, they need these things to keep on with what they do do.

I know these places, I say. I look around my breast front with my finger for money being in an institution brings for a while. It isn't real money anyway, money that I make or must keep. Two please, I say. As long as I don't have to be present.

Two is good. They're giving away hams and a Frigidaire at this one. You could use a Frigidaire.

He is looking at the hole in my trailer where glass should be that I have plugged with bags you can see through. I have this trailer for free because of that hole. But I know he is not really looking that long into my trailer because he is casting his eyes down again over the shelf of my bosom where the money came from, and it isn't so much the money he is interested in.

He gives me my chances.

I put them up on the board with the others, move a tack off one, and stick the two under it.

He puts my money in a clip, then in his pocket.

The kids giggle from somewhere, one, then two of them.

He grabs the aerial where it has been lying between the green bottles of my bottle garden, and turns to face the giggling so fast the aerial slaps him. This causes him to say many things which the kids, although used to hearing a lot of everything, stop giggling to hear and thereby, with their silence as a frame, give themselves and their whereabouts away. Ernie's off with the next giggle, tearing through the court like his buttoned-down pants pocket spouts fire.

His leaving fast like that, aerial whipping, dislodges some of the chances tacked to my door. There they go, in flight out over the fence that is so full of other stuff that the wind here works to stick to it, but the chances don't stop and stick, they fluff up and go off over the gully.

It is the gully where the cows stand, with the wild girl.

2

THE GULLY IS ALL PROMISE: the sky dips in everywhere and what grows in it doesn't have to be planted, all those blue flowers and black-eyed flowers and flowers with thorns at the base and big green prickly bunches in a sword shape that aren't cactus but look like something an old lady would tend, in a size Small though, in a pot.

I am no old lady. I just wear that kind of clothes. Where I was before, that was all they had the day they said I should go and good luck. That is, sweaters with holes, a sundress that the hem has let go of, a skirt with hooks to close. You would think with all the years people spend there, at first always younger, that all they would have to give out would be a young person's clothes. I do remember all of my young person's personals going into a bag with a slip with my name written on it, I remember that, but maybe they are careful not to give back what you gave because the clothes make the man or woman. Instead they mix them up and give them out to other people so you get more courage or less confusion than with your own. But who am I now is the question. Who is a woman in a sundress with a lot of hem? They might as well give me the slip with the name on it too, the one the clothes belong to, rather than let me be somebody in clothes that go with no one.

Sometimes clothes like mine, castoffs, get stuck to the fence beside the gully, but more often what sticks is a lot of plastic. Plastic sticks well, and then wind pushes it tight to the wire like it will soften the barb or like it has found a home. Then more plastic hits it and shreds, then grays, or sometimes it is already black, and soon you have a fence all tufted, almost like a quilt that a cow would have no fear to mount and climb over, or at least stick her head through and eat wild, a trailer flower or a bush in season.

There in the gully, those cows eating move very much like clouds, sometimes a lot of them together like it is a cloud party, or everybody is far and near, spread out like nobody wants to talk. Sometimes the clouds hang up on the windmill tank, dipping their fronts in water that is pumped up, but mostly they drift down because of the press of the gully and the gravity those steep sides insist on, the sides that keep the water in.

I am always looking at the gully and especially at the cows, but today I am walking into it, leaving my cinderblock behind and the fence with its inches thick of plastic and old clothes that is my job to clean on Tuesday, which should be coming up any day now. I don't stop this walking of mine until gravity gets me and makes me run headlong.

I almost don't know how. My shoes are old lady shoes, which make how even more hard. But gravity does help.

And the wild one.

She is in with the cows, where I am going. She has gone and pressed herself up against this cloudy bunch of cows. The cows spooked when I ran into the gully before, the cows jerked their heads up and ran themselves out of their cloud until I saw her, but then I stopped. This time I will not stop.

I have waited.

Now the cows are almost used to me. They sidestep and stop chewing is all when I run in, they have to be slapped on their hineys to get going out of the way, to get bunched up and show her to me.

But they won't.

They turn their heads when I ask, Where is she? As if I am making her up, as if they don't know. *Ee-haw,* I say then, the way you are supposed to, with cows on TV who don't do what you want. They just turn their heads away again, this time down to the grass, and go on chewing.

I walk back, sneaking looks, yes, but still I have to watch where I am going with these old lady shoes and still I have to stop at the rise and look across.

The fence can hardly keep the court in with all the left-over Airstreams and abandoned unrentables and tool sheds that people use for relatives, and parts, and the pretend stuff trailers are stuck with and then there's old string tangled with tumbleweed or beer webbing, tires chopped up where water catches, propane valves and cut inner tubes, and my trailer. When I go past the chicken counter in the supermarket I think of the court from here: whole fryers by the gate, the quartered alongside the gutter, and the parts, wings and legs in stiff packages out close to the gully and its fence. I guess mine is the little bag of innards, with just a heart and a few other things good for being fried up but not much else.

But of course if you look at how the court measures up to the rest of the county spread out past it, the town, for example, trying so hard to stop cars that drive by on the skinny little highway, you can hardly think of the court as the chicken section, which is so important in a market that it gets Grade A and colored posters over it. No, the court is the part of the town that has petered out, where maybe it was once a place where people lived to fix things for you cheap or clean but now is where the town has pulled away from, with some miles standing in between. There is even a bend between the town and the court that prevents anything anymore petering out to the town or someone in the town ever having to stare into it.

The bend is also for the weather. If the weather is good, then the sun just sets on it nice and red and that's that. But if it rains so much or the snow melts somewhere else so fast runoff comes down here like down a trough, then this bend with its pushed-up sides that keeps the town from having to look at the court is a help—it keeps the town from drowning.

As for the court, if the weather is ever that bad, it will drown. This I can tell. The court is where the water will be if it pushes over the island the bend has made. When this happens, the antenna trees will not reach the top to mark the spot of the court, rescue people will have to swim under the water when it is not too wild to find the trailer anchors at the bottom, my bottle garden in its circle will be like a big plug that won't work, and the swings from the swingset will float way over the top bar.

I have time to think these things out because I am waiting for the cows to relax and move their cloud around so when and if I turn, I will see her, I will catch her out.

Whenever I don't watch, it happens.

There she is, and there she is not, the cows giving her red shirt or sweater room and then squeezing it out of sight just like that.

All I see is that she is not looking at me. It is like an accident that I see her at all. I almost try not to look because then I see more.

I run at the cows again. I stumble in my too big shoes over the heels and over clumps of brush, and I run anyway, then I kick them off and run. I run into the stickers, and I run anyway.

And she is there, a little girl in red with no shoes and her hair all stuck out, fine like mine.

The cows are silent, the kind of silence cows make between chews, between a gulp and a vomit, when they're looking at you like you are the dumb one so you can't keep on looking. Then the cows step back into their cloud and step away, and she is gone.

3

I'M HUNCHED, WRIGGLING ON shoes, when I see the grape-drink-colored hairclip in a scuzz of thistle. Precious metal is what I suppose, some kind of jewel-in-the-raw. I brush off the crow that is thinking *stray silver gum wrap*, I flick dirt off the clip and take a look. When I see it's what it is, in regular rows too wide-spaced for the thin kind of hair I have, I put it in my pocket anyway.

I take it out again going back, the way you do with something new to you, and I figure out why it really won't hold: the teeth are melted, something very hot has pressed into it. I can't imagine why.

4

THE BOY NEEDING HELP with his aim throws down his rock and shouts, Collin! so Collin will miss. But he doesn't and glass goes all over and the sound is great, nothing but great. Even the baby stops howling after the sound. For this, Collin turns around and bends in the middle in a real bow to let everyone know he knows he is what's great, then he starts waving his arms like they are about to fall off at the joint to tell them he sees she is coming.

She is Kate.

I know her name from the Kate! Kate! she is yelled at half the night, and I can hear Kate even before Collin sees her. I am sitting in a place in the gully that no one bothers because it is up by where kids play, a good place to see the sled that

Kate pulls, which bangs over the rocks, a sled that is large and out-of-season slow. White dust from the kind of rock that's under us powders up onto the two snakes on top so they look snow-covered and right for a sled. They bounce and nearly come off as the sled crashes from outcrop to outcrop, as noisy as the glass breaking.

But there are really only so many bottles that nobody wants, only so many that don't give back a nickel. The one that still stands after Collin hits at them is cracked in the back and just falls apart when the boy who is Freddie at last finds a loose rock to tap it.

Kate hoists herself up the last outcrop, with her sled and snakes still behind.

How'd you make those snakes set up so quiet? asks Collin.

She doesn't say right away. After all, Collin is her brother. He doesn't look like her brother but never mind. He asks again and adds, This one looks dead, and gives it his toe. The snake wriggles for it.

I put them in a jar in the freezer, she says as she swings the sled a little at the end so the snakes look up.

They are so much alike, says Freddie who has just left his shattered bottle glass. Maybe they are one snake cut in two.

Kate nods like she agrees but says nothing to his talk about how they would look inside out. They're sisters, she says.

Maybe Freddie will kiss one, says Collin.

Freddie uses his stick on him and then a shove for good measure.

Well, now, says Collin, who has fallen spread-eagled on the sled in pretend self-protection, I see the snakes have all moved off, taken their rattles and gone. All we got left here is a sled. My sled, I believe.

Jesus Christ alive, says Kate. You know whose sled this is and it is mine now.

The baby who has been eating dirt between stone throws and bottle breaks, whose face is blistered with snot, grey and old, yells gibberish to support her. Kate goes to him, trailing the sled, not letting what she has towed so far get taken by the boys.

Look, he's sitting in his own wet, she says, and he is. She moves him and puts the sled over the wet part and sits on it, bottomlipping Collin so he knows who's sitting. But the sled slides where the grass thins, where white rock shows itself through at a slope, it slips and glides a little down that wet grass and rock, with her on it.

Freddie is smashing whatever glass Collin hasn't smaller and smaller. Come here, says Kate. Collin, you come too.

The glass is all broken anyway.

Pee here, she says, moving the sled a little, pointing with her pelvis.

Collin's smile starts and he takes out his pee-er.

Come on, calls Kate to Freddie. It will be fun. Put your pee right here. We need it.

Freddie says nothing but keeps his hand over his fly.

How about a candy? says Kate. Please?

Not for candy from a bag, says Freddie. Not that kind of candy.

Candy from plants up here that I made, says Kate, not candy that has been bought.

Kate brings out a kiss-wrapper from her shirt pocket and unpeels one end. What's inside is grey and pulpy, homemade. It's here, she says. She puts it on a rock. You can eat it when.

She squats and pulls her pants down under her skirt so you can't see a thing and pees just where Collin and the baby have. When she's all rearranged, she picks up the candy again and puts it to her lips.

Freddie snatches the dirty homemade wad from her and eats it, wrapper and all, then unzips so quick in a turn that no one, not even Collin, can see, not that he would, Collin rolling with his laughs on the ground.

There's a flood after they've all done it.

Okay, says Kate. Just a little more. She spits.

They all finish it off with spit because really Freddie can spit good and Kate spitting just makes him want to try.

That's what they say.

All right, says Kate when the place is juicy wet. All right, and she moves the sled back over it. Then the two boys punch each other for the front until she says it is her idea anyway, and Collin looks over the edge and says, Kate, maybe you can sit here and even if it's not your sled. Then the baby starts to cry because who can give him enough room since the sled is really only good for three, but they shift him and Collin does the push and the scramble and they go.

Since the sled is never going anywhere, I don't say Stop, I don't stand and say, That's dangerous, because you know they are going to frown and are liable to kick. I finger that hairclip I found, I lean way out. After its spitty, pissy quick start, the sled sets down the gully good, as if what slicks the runners is a wax they go so fast. They go so fast their teeth smack together, each one, and their bones bump—I can hear it. I run after them, up and down the gully's parts.

The baby doesn't cry after the start, it is that fast, it is so straight down, bouncing over yucca as if it is a plant you could bounce over, scraping the limestone sides of bare bunches of rock so hard the white comes off in clouds. Gravity sucks them down one rough patch after another and then to a crack over a really sharp drop, this one mostly filled in with old car parts and wheels to cars, and that's where they come to rest.

And rest it is that the sled comes to and comes apart at,

where their eyes are all about knocked out and their hearing is nothing but what big machines make between gears, and they don't seem to even be breathing.

Kate in front who has had nothing to hold onto, just the rag that tows the sled, has sailed free so far forward into the cows lifting their heads, into their soft sides presented in amongst the car parts, that she doesn't put out her arms to stop herself. Does she want to break up those cows, and when they shift does she see—like I do—a flash of red? the red of sky? her own blood? of a sweater?

Once they are stopped and I am standing with my hands at my sides like a crow, in that eerie slow bunch of seconds when they all look as if they are dead for sure, limbs and heads and arms all wrong, and white dust coming up like they are already in heaven, Kate says to get out of the way, she's coming through. She wobbles up to the crashed sled and jerks at its rag until the others gasp and then say how fun it was, let's go again, all but the baby who sets its mouth in a shriek, seeing me.

5

ERNIE WANTS TO GET MORE than money out of me, he wants the whole hog, he sees through the see-through of my sundress and addresses it with the wonder of a boy caught by a color catalogue.

Now, I have had kids. They have come out of me, dragging any leftover girl of me with them, so I can't say that I have been locked up in a closet all my life with nothing going on in the free will department unless being bombarded by hormones, *whore moans* as I hear boys call it who are pretending to study, skips the free will part. I had those kids. They won't have me now, but that is beside the point.

I forget about Ernie and his wants when I clean the fence. It is Tuesday, and it is not easy cleaning this fence with your bare fingers so I have devised a way of using whatever I pull off as a glove around my hands for the next bit of barb and pliers and knife, but sometimes this glove slips and there the barbs are, waiting to snag me as much as anything. I get cut.

Blood coming out in a stream deserves a sleeve. I won't lick it like a wild thing, I just won't.

The red matches the red on the fence's other side. I see her again. She has a cup that she is tossing skyward and missing, catching, but never breaking it too. Either she doesn't throw it far or it's not broken because it's plastic, a toy. I like the idea that it is a toy because she is a child and what can she do all day but starve or play?

The cows cover her, the cup pops up out of their covering.

What feeds her? Grasshops? The stray pork bone? These are not milk cows with oozing organs. No fruit tree or cornfield or vegetable patch casts off food for twenty miles. I think I can say that for sure because these are not garden-planting people. My bottles are the best that is planted here.

But she eats. She must eat.

And she plays.

The cup lands on the broad back of a lead cow until the cow shakes it free as if a fly is standing on its back. Then the cup comes up again.

I am working down the fence, filling up my bag with all

the tufted trash it gives, thinking again of Ernie and his wants and the cup that marks her wants—or is it just play with both of them?—when I stop in front of the trailer next to mine. One of the kids is face front inside the widest window, looking out.

Kate, I can tell. She is the one tall enough to see out the window without falling forward, the couch against the window being at such an angle.

A little closer and I can see by her eyes what she's watching.

The cup goes up.

I watch her watch. She doesn't see me yet, my hands lying quiet and still at the barb. Her eyes are not on the fence with me but watch past that, as far as the cows. And the cup.

Someone's middle moves in beside Kate. Kate moves her mouth in talk but not much of it after that middle moves in. Then she is hit by the arm beside that middle. I can tell because she jerks forward and her face changes to all surprise and quick-closed eyes, then she wriggles off the couch, head down so nothing like tears can show.

But not before she sees me and I see her see me.

Were they playing, a nod from one releases the cup from the other, or the cup thrown three times means something?

I decide I know. I decide one of the girls is a kind of sister to the other, the kind that doesn't depend on blood necessarily but could, I think, or depends on a sled that one girl gives to the other.

The cows disperse, each to its far corner, and no one is there again behind them but there's still the cup which is tilted to the air so the dirt or rain can get in.

Rain will fall out of the grey that has caught on the clouds that hang less above than on this fence that I face. The clouds also hang on the bend in the road that doesn't protect the court and its trailers or the cows and the small red-covered girl who hides with them.

I cut myself again on the barb on the bottom rung which is a good-for-nothing rung made by someone who is out to surprise kneeling cows or creatures that scuttle under, or me. This time the red is the little girl on my hand and I lick it.

6

DAYS, KATE'S MOTHER SITS ON the step to the door and watches the hills hump toward the sun, watches between stop-bys of men, watches the cows reposition themselves in some dark or light of these hills.

But does she watch for the one I do?

It is not official, the girl going off, the way the mother doesn't call in some others to look, a helicopter maybe. If you don't report, who's to say what or who's missing? She isn't much for anyone asking. In a dream that I have, the mother comes with her head down like a dog and then turns away without a whine or a word.

That is her in life.

Maybe some high school thing happened because she is young and not even plain-looking but better, although she wears glasses. The glasses are what brings to mind the school, big glasses in the style they have, windshield style so the whole eye is looking at you, not just the frame and the eyebrows, so you see her eyes must see a lot.

I am only a few years older than she is, I can tell by the way our faces are made and are unmaking. I don't have enough life in me yet from where I was to feel the want tendrils coming out of me, the cut ones and the new ones, looking for ways to hold on, to call on her. Other ladies call on her and her phone number must be written in many bathrooms because men do come and go, talk loud and drink, judging from the number of beer bottles the kids take and break up and the others which I find and thrust down into my garden.

To go with these glasses she does crosswords. I have picked them off the fence by her place, in a small script and with all the boxes filled in, even the abbreviations, the short-fors and the early Greek which only a crossword person will keep track of.

Kids don't bother her place much even though she has her own. Kids catch on other places, they snap or swirl in and out at will, no one having the will to stem them. Kate and

Collin and the baby come out early and tear around with the others, stand under eaves when it rains or go elsewhere. None of the others drag over their pieces of toys to play. There, the only good-sized toy that is not from a cereal box is in the way of the trailer and is the busted-up sled, not even a bike or a three-wheeler, and that sled is broken now for a while.

When the kids come like cats to try to drag off my table or fold and unfold my chair or even pull out all the plastic from the picture-window side of the trailer, I ask about the cows and the girl and who she looks like. All they agree on is that she looks like me. I think that is because of the cookies I lay out in a line across the checked tablecloth that the boy shows me how to play checkers with. You see, you eat off the tops so the icing is opposite and you also eat what you jump. When they play like that they will say anything, the way a cat will, given milk in a saucer out a window it can't open.

The mother does leave the key for the kids when she doesn't come home. And they almost always have shoes with Velcro closings and usually both of them, and bright-colored so they're not like bugs under a bed going to bite you for losing them. And she does buy milk because the jugs sit in front, in clumps, measuring rain like something scientific, every day a new answer.

The sun is going down behind those jugs in the quiet of what to some is the business end of the day but here it is often when the cock crows. There is a canary next door which is too exhausted to make noise every real dawn because the lady doesn't cover it. Some days it won't even sing. Maybe it won't sing also because she sometimes leaves the gas on, which is bad for birds. This woman lights her smokes on the stove and forgets it. I have seen this when she leaves the door open in the middle of talking and laughing with the mother next door, with the stove hissing behind them.

We don't speak yet, this woman and I or the mother. However, there was this jello salad day, when all the court women mixed together old leftovers like they were fresh and stirred in fancy nuts and bolts—walnuts and celery—to spot a wild cherry or lime or orange jello shaking on a sheet cake pan, and all to impress each other. Instead of eating it, they took just little bites on their plates as if it were poison. I myself put out a dish with pretzels mixed with some of that pretend whip, making it a food for after dinner that is not really dessert, but simple enough. People like to think they are not really eating something and that is what this dish gives the effect of. In this case, they really didn't eat it so I had quite a main course for a time.

After the food part of the day, we washed up and someone tried to sell Avon or Amway, something with an A. The woman with the A-product standing up in front of us looked as cool as anything at the start of her talk. You could see someone had told her we would leave big bills at her feet and be thankful, but where there were blanks in her speech that she was supposed to fill in with things especially for us she had to stop. That stopping was what pulled all of us down, the filling in of blanks that we couldn't help her with. Where exactly did we fit in those big blanks that said what we should buy? The ladies around me were current on all the arguments people have over surrogate sex or their beating their mothers on TV but the tuck is all out of them at the commercials, they don't even bother to surf them. This is what I see through their windows with me sitting outside at night, not watching anything but the shadows the TV lights make, these lights that have been bounced all the way from the stars.

At that party I wore what I came in, one of the uniforms but with the name all picked off, with nothing that said where or what number. The color of it is a bad green and tight in the armpits, it being maybe a man's really, the top a little dartless. You know how ladies are, they sometimes don't see the person inside as anything other than filling, and if the wrapper is spoiled, well. Or maybe I smiled wrong that day. I put on this smile to get out, the one that convinced them that I could go out and try again, but now it's hard to get rid of, it's the one that tries too hard to get out, the one that people back off from. But who goes for a frown or a face that's pulled blank?

When I see the mother on her step watching, I want to come over and watch her, but because of the party, I don't think so. I do go and stand way behind her to see if her head is pointed at the cows the way mine is but she moves or leaves when I get there even though I am very quiet.

The girl doesn't always wear red. When I ask what color she is in today, the lady with the quiet canary turns from me quick as if she's doing what she should to answer. Some other colors she wears sometimes but the red makes it easier for me to see her in and around the cows and once, where there is a tree, red in the tree, and in the rain, red under the cows. I can point to the red and say, See now? but usually the girl sees me pointing and her red is gone like that.

Or the person won't look.

I say it is good luck to look, go on. I'll bet you can't look. You can look better than me with my plasticked-up window.

It is a day when only wind is keeping rain from falling straight down, when I forget the jello welcome and walk over to ask the mother what I am always wanting to ask her. Even before she doesn't answer, I can see her eyes aren't right, they're asleep-awake eyes, and that high school look of hers is sucked now into pinpoints inside her head where the cheering has stopped, or can't be stopped. I have seen this where I was before, and the lines to get rid of it are long.

But I know this mother is the one because that cup that is thrown among the cows is part of a set that sits in pieces around her place, all the toys that replace the sled.

Or else the kids left it there.

7

In the institution hung a picture I did not look at. It hung like a tumbleweed caught against the wall, a dark scrawl of who knows whose history tangled up that could get out if you looked too hard at it. Instead of looking at it, I heard about it in stories from the others. I had to hear, they told me even when I stopped up my ears, people who ate their hoarded treats in my room, people who bounced balls at me, even the ones who slipped me white pills without their paper cups. They would tell me fifty people are lined up in that picture in the very old dress of the institution, and the spindly trees behind them glow bare with the land that is spread out under them, and just as bare. The building is mostly a dugout, what people put up first when they go to a frontier or get thrown out, a dugout that is not, at least, dug down like a grave but sideways, with the deaths ahead and deaths behind. That's what they said.

I know the insides of institutions well, how they smell so clean they hurt the throat, and I know their everyday ways, the people in them who cry like it is a place they have to have until food is brought or the stomach pumped and then they complain. I know a lot about the people who wear white outfits to keep themselves away from anyone who is actually their job in the institution, people who like to touch with gloves on.

But like some who can't keep out of jails, I can't resist the solemn signing in, though the first time it was a mistake. But I was ready. All those years before, moving from parent to parent, made me ready for an institution and its ways, because those parents, well. One of them did want me so I had a baby but then of course I couldn't stay, I had to go away and take that baby with me and then of course there were no more parents but me. After that I knew a man whose huskiness sounded Indian to me, like a voice that had chanted into the wind so much it had gone hoarse. But he went away, taking that hoarseness that might or might not have been from chanting—maybe whiskey—and leaving me with another baby that I couldn't have, unless it were one for the protection of the other.

I was institution-ready.

I wasn't in an institution when I heard about the cat. Ernie told me about the cat. We were just two together then when he was ten, and these were new parents for him too at this place which was no institution, which was a family. His cat, he said, chased cars, his cat would jump on car roofs and land on the hood and then stretch out clear to safety. Tonight his cat would come from a cloud and go back into it after it ate all of what was set out in front of me and Ernie, the grease on that plate going white after a whole night of our sitting. That cat, he said, was not one of the pussies that lap milk in a dish but one they like to stuff if they can, its paws pigeon-toed, cats that leave fat prints in plaster in exhibits before they escape anyway. And this cat is always hungry, yes it is, and it will come and eat everything on our plates if we can tell it our names, our real true names. Otherwise it will eat us. What will you say to it? he asks me.

A dog was howling to get us in this home, it howled as if it was hungry too but not for leftovers. You can answer, I said. You can say.

He told me he had a real name and a place and a trailer court he could collect when he was old enough to, that his mother had died and his father went off so his grandfather had this court he could get.

It was quite a bit more than envy I felt. I felt he was just like one of the children in these homes who knows where the milk is and pours it. I couldn't listen to him anymore, I just put my head down next to my plate and closed my eyes.

The cat didn't come and it seemed when I woke up I was already signing for my watch and some other piece of jewelry you don't hardly miss after they put you in an institution. Ernie was in the foyer collecting chances for a Sunbeam blender and asking me as I walked out in my new sundressed self, if I wanted one without recognizing me, saying I needed a chance. I said, Don't I know you?

I doubt it, he said, and I knew right away what he meant. I didn't know those two of mine I had had to leave with parents who had diaper pins, and Ernie with sideburns, those grown-old shoulders and starched-up white shirts, was hardly Ernie at the dinner plate that first night.

He didn't remember a cat. With wings? he at least asked. But he took me with him anyway. It must have been the way I told him, hiking up my straps, how I didn't care about the cat. Or maybe it was how I said it, spitting like a sister.

8

QUE SERA, SERA, HE SINGS, this large man hanging onto a small bouquet. Who brings bought flowers to a court? The large man hides these flowers in their white cuff of bought paper behind his back and has since he parked his long slim station wagon with *Lyle's Locks* painted across it, front door to back. This man comes sashaying with his flowers past my place, that is, he walks right up and sings his song loud, singing it right up to the mother's door as if he owns it. And he doesn't ring her bell the way the other men do, he just keeps on singing loud.

The door opens pop! like a can of turned fruit. The mother just falls all over him, she takes those flowers and hugs him and kisses him with kisses that would peel the socks off a sailor, which he is not though his arm wears the blue bruise of tattoos, of flower and coil. Kids who are not hers wash up out of the swell of the others and stare. The kids who are hers, hide their eyes.

Pardon me, Ma'am, he says, after air. Have I come to the right place?

You bet your sweethearted ass, says the mother. Where have you been for an entire thirty-four-and-a-half days? What took you so long to deliver those lock gizmos?

He gives her a look made out of tin. That is, all her kisses have polished him up good but he's still hard and smooth and changeable. You can see him start to change, how all the song is gone out of his next words: It was thirty days exact.

They are parted now, two steps from each other, so words can be held back. And they are, so far back. At last he reaches into his pocket and says, Here, this is for them. Sweets. He yields up a brown bag that no kid steps up to take.

Collin, says the mother. You get that.

They go on in the door after that, she already in a spoon shape for him, you can see it in the way she turns so close to his shirt, the way she reaches around him for the latch, the way she dodges that now no-song voice with the back of her head, the way she then buries her face into the bouquet as she pulls the door shut so who could not see the size of it and how it smells so sweet?

All those kids, hers and others, stand outside at a distance from the trailer as if it will soon start to rock so much they might get crushed. They bury their faces in their shirts and sniff for *eau d'flower*. They sniff the old, used-up grass, then they go back to their shirts. Out of motion for a change, they talk soft, all in one place.

But the baby cries, the baby they can never keep hushed. And when the man opens the door, barechested, the baby is still bawling. The man holds a bottle of milk in one hand and a bottle of whiskey in the other, with a long lighted cigar in that other to help him point. He points at the kids, the smoke of the cigar coming out around his face when he talks. It is a young-old face, one that high school girls like, thinking they are getting what their age deserves, which is true but not good for them when they grow up, which is soon with a face like that. He points at the kids with his cigar and asks them which hand do they choose for which bottle, and whichever one they do, he cuffs them.

The baby goes silent quick. The baby doesn't want to be picked next to choose because he can't, especially if Kate and Collin can't, Kate and Collin who don't run away like the others after their cuffs because where would they run?

Did you miss me? the man asks Kate. Did you miss every single thing about me?

Kate doesn't say.

The man walks over to his car and opens the front part painted on with *Lyle's Locks* and brings out groceries. On the way back, with sacks in both arms, he gathers up the baby. The baby starts wailing again and throws himself into a wild wriggling to get down. The man clenches his teeth around his cigar and whacks the baby on what bottom he can reach, given the groceries. An orange falls from the top of a sack in the middle of the whacking. It rolls as far as my card table, the baby bawling, Ball! Ball! among other things, as it rolls.

Kate runs to pick it up.

I pick it up first since it is under my feet.

Kate's hand is there when I pick it up, so I drop the orange into it.

Ma'am, he says, shifting that baby into a better grip and taking the orange from Kate and dropping it right to the ground again. Dirty, he says to Kate.

He means me.

The baby starts up again with fresh cries, louder because you can see he wanted that orange. And his cries only get louder again, you can tell because after he's gone inside, it's still as loud.

I put my dishes into a pot on top of my card table, and I wash them, one at a time, I slowly wash them in the water of that pot. Then I get a stick and fetch the orange out from far under my trailer where it has rolled and I wash it off under the tap that I have outside.

The orange is my dessert. I peel it and eat it. I am still very hungry and an orange is not the rice and furred bread and soft carrot I'm stuck with, day to day, along with food for cats. No, I don't hesitate, I eat every section of that orange, every dry and pits-ful section. The left torn peelings glow on my table.

The trailers face this way and that, mostly around the place where you put quarters in machines that either wash clothes or dry them, which is also the place where you bang at buttons to make flippers bounce balls against gravity and in and out of cups under glass, but trailers do face away. So some of the court could have seen me gather the bright peels, just as they could have seen the way the man looked so hungry at those children.

But I doubt it.

9

CABLE RUNS ALL OVER THE PLACE. It's snarled and cut and weltered in with sixteen other snakes of various breeds, all black, and all of them mating at the base of a pole, which could be telephone if that line laying across the top of the pre-built were attached to anything which it sure doesn't seem to be, this being the last pole in the neighborhood.

I'm whistling some deadbeat sixties song I can't get the high notes of, raking the leaves all around those cables and wires and all the whatnot that gets caught in such a snarl, and I've almost moved on when a man inside the trailer which abuts the cable comes out, a man with a scar up one side of his smile like a pumpkin carved and left off.

You had better know what you're doing, trash lady, he

says. Because if you fool around here too much, I lose it. My power is what I'm talking about. You stick that rake where it oughtn't to be and off it will go.

He doesn't smooth his scar into a smile.

I move my rake on. These people will get friendly over time I think, even though they are not like gypsies who have family in their wanderings, all crisscrossed like a puzzle mated in amongst each other so they are always a help in some way, if only for more children. But the court people have to have at least some gypsy in them to want to live in this kind of place and that is why they will get friendly.

I hooked it up myself, says the man, following me. Don't you go fouling it up.

The man follows me and my raking all the way to the steps of the pregnant teenager who does not look up from her school book when the man wags his finger into a point, either at her or me. Then the man turns back, because of this teenager not looking? or me with my raking going on? and says all the rest of his Don't come backs under his heavy breath.

I keep raking.

Children play tug-o-war with someone's sweater, with that someone standing by, crying.

The pinball man works his game outside, right up next to where all the laundry suds gush out in big grey clots into the gully. He hulks way over the electronics so when I go for the transparent papers that candy is sometimes wrapped in and is always tossed and sticky with an invisible fluttering that could collect on his huge purple and grey shoes that are supposed to be for running but instead support the arching that he makes scoring pinball points, shoes he doesn't so much as lift as lean into while his hands and head are doing other things, when I rake he doesn't even notice my clawing across his shoes for the wrapper.

Ernie is counting the stubs of his chance books, stapled blunt knots of paper all so carefully numbered, some tied with elastic, some with clips. Goddammit, lady, he says as I rake up a loose chance that twists in with the candy paper and wire and dirt. But he doesn't bend down to dislodge it, nor does he take it back when I offer it to him, he just lets the chance go, he waves it off with more counting.

The mechanic is nailing a Bible to his front porch rail and putting birdseed on it. There is not much to the porch except for kindling and lathe, but now the Bible has made it square. The birdseed falls to the ground, most of it, because it is shaken out in the blind way of the mechanic whose eyes are greased shut forever for looking too much into the inside bottoms of cars. I rake up the extra birdseed with all the rest. Birds don't wear clothes, he says to me, or to anyone.

I rake on.

I stop at the back end of my place where the fence is almost fallen through, where it leans drunk and low and few things catch on it, and there I sort out my bunch of rakings, smooth the birdseed over the ground, and sit.

The cows below haul themselves around in their cloud or clouds, they move one bite at a time, some down in the gully and some in one of the folds. All of them match, a white splotch on each face front. What does that splotch mean? I hear a doctor ask where I have been let out of. Why, spilled drugs, I say, why, a mother's milk wasted, why, I say, a cow's face. Electricity, the doctor writes down, three times a day, and sedate her.

Thank god, this electricity almost doesn't reach here where the cows stand. They keep it spooled up in the plant and when it's let out here it's the last of the line and it goes dodging and limping on into corners and sometimes runs completely out of energy, putt-putts right to a stop.

Same with the land. It's wild land in this middle part. It refused people and their doings for a million years and only now is when we can stay a little. It's so wild and useless only birds with extra-wide wings have been over the whole place, nobody but birds bother to keep track of all this middle wildness.

The land won't have anything to do with anything else. Look at it, there's no sub-basement, no pipes of below-ground swimming pools that could take it and make it tame. You can see where they sent out a spur of the railroad right to where the tracks of it curl up as if it had a seizure trying to couple over this kind of land. If you go far enough in, you can see those rails and no roads at all, nothing to set up the land like an ordinary land, to take you from here to somewhere where things are different.

This is what Ernie tells me.

Thirty-three, thirty-four, a boy sings out. Thirty-five.

Kate is on me, hard-breathing, her head and hands whipping past all the cinderblock that won't hide her, she comes for me.

The boy says, Forty-five.

Kate ducks behind my block, pulls in her feet but her head comes up. Then she crouches and sneaks off.

Forty-eight.

She comes back to my feet, her head behind my leg.

Fifty.

I take out one of the wrapped candies I find lying around in the court. Some candy is always lying around here.

Here I come, he says. Ready or not.

I hold the candy in front of Kate's face. You leave her out there, I say like it is a fact she knows.

Kate doesn't touch the candy.

The boy crashes around the next nearby trailer to look behind an old mirror with a starburst break.

It doesn't matter, you leaving her, I say, my own two kids left me.

Kate sucks in snot.

The boy stops to tie his shoe, his head arching over the laces every second or so to check to see if she moves anywhere, to decide on his next move.

I find a restaurant sweet deeper in my pocket, one of the free loose ones that make dinner remembered better or forgotten, the kind that chip and get old-looking fast but still smell like sweet chalk. Will you help me catch her is all? I offer it to her with my hand curled around it.

She takes it.

She don't want to be catched, she whispers around the wet of her mouth and the candy.

The boy, who is Freddie, starts throwing rocks, tired of not finding her. The rocks skip over to where we sit. I put my skirt over Kate, her whole self.

Freddie follows his rocks. I heard you talking, he says.

I am a crazy person, don't you know that? I say.

Talking to yourself, he says, walking all the way around me.

Kate gasps, terror leaking.

What was that? he asks, bending lower, not having the guts to lift my skirt.

I ate baloney today. Or catfood. I don't remember which.

Freddie takes a step away from me. No, he says.

They are both hard to digest.

He's already turned back to the court, hands over his mouth, pretend-gagging, then running.

I find that barrette in my pocket, its grape stumps. What about your Dad—doesn't he want her? I ask as Kate undrapes herself.

Don't ask me nothing, says Kate. She looks hard at this barrette and calls out, I'm free, I'm free.

I tuck the barrette away and eat the first candy, peel it and suck on it, then I take up my rake, bend down to loosen whatever's caught in its teeth.

Eight, says Kate. Nine.

10

I BELIEVE I GOT THEM ALL, says McGuire, who slaps the leftover pencils across his shiny star so hard it's as if he is believing what he says with all his heart.

The sheriff nods, on parade, the cherrytop blink-blinking as fast as he makes his footfalls in front of the children who are lined up and silly alongside the court entrance, silly with pencils.

I got enough to do catching crooks, he says, and keeping the town from wrack and ruin without having to run down you kids for the school.

The children poke each other with the blunt ends of the new pencils. Some work at chewing off the opposite ends.

Ernie, you got them all out of the bathroom and out from under all your units?

Ernie nods along with the head of his big flashlight which is still on.

I guess you got enough violations, you don't need this one, says the sheriff, chuckling.

Ernie chuckles too, then he turns off his light.

Okay. The sheriff stoops to pick up a board loaded with clipped-on papers lying half inside his blinking car, then he straightens up to ask with his pencil and his patience, How many is all, McGuire?

I had twenty, says McGuire. I got ten pencils left. That's how many?

The children swordfight with their new pencils, they drum.

Come on now, which one of you knows?

I hold up both hands with all the fingers out so the children can see.

The children don't see.

They got to go to school, sheriff, says McGuire. Some of them are pretty old to be so backward. He is shaking his head and putting up his fingers and beginning One, two—

Ten, McGuire. It's ten. Up a couple from last year. The sheriff makes a mark on the paper clipped closest to the top of the board. You people move in and out so fast that if I don't put you in my facilities, I can't keep track of you.

The parents or just bystanders drawn by the cherrytop

blinking step back or slink off a step or look away or shrug, So what?

I expect each and every one of your kids on the bus on Monday morning, you hear? the sheriff goes on. And if you kids are not in school, you're in trouble. Remember that—in school or in trouble. Get them there or I'll send McGuire in after you.

McGuire shakes his cuffs which are hooked onto a frayed loop and clank as fierce as cans on a scarecrow.

The children stick their pencils up their noses.

That's the whole business, says the sheriff, scooting his papers and their clip back into the back seat of the car that is still blinking. You parents, he says over the door window after he straightens up, remember, we see them at the bus at six forty-five sharp.

His hand is already on the door to shut it and McGuire is already slamming his shut when I come out of that bunch of parents and say into the doorcrack, You forgot one.

What? says the sheriff. He turns to McGuire. She says you forgot one. Did you forget one?

McGuire sticks his head out his window and points at each one he can point to. The rest are playing tag with their pencils, running and whacking each other with their new pencil tips. McGuire clears his throat and throws open his door and steps out again, hoisting his pants, shifting his gun and cuffs so the sheriff can see how hard this counting completely over will be. I don't know, says McGuire, I think it's the same as before.

You can ask her about it, I say and point to the mother whose back is turned, who is almost gone around the side of the first trailer.

Ma'am, asks the sheriff with his voice raised to make the distance, what do you know about there being more kids, a miscount if that's what she says we have here?

The mother does stop but since she is already so far away the sheriff has to raise his voice again. Didn't I tell all of you to bring every single last one of your kids down here? Didn't you tell them, Ernie?

I did. I told them, says Ernie.

You know, says the sheriff, we need cooperation here, a lot of it.

They're all here as far as I know, says Ernie.

They all turn toward the mother.

The mother picks up the baby who doesn't squall until she whips him up to her, until she says, The girl's gone with her father to visit her Uncle Jim and that is all.

That's not so, I say. That's just not so. She's down there with the cows. There, I say, with my arm stretched out toward the gully-side.

She's the trash lady, officers, says the mother, shushing the baby.

So? asks the sheriff. She says there's another kid here we didn't count. Now is there or isn't there?

The baby lights into a real riff of screaming as if it is being pinched. The lady is looney, says the mother over him. She sees things. She's nuts.

I stick my tongue out at her.

The sheriff says, Ernie? and Ernie steps into the fray that he and his big flashlight have been staying out of, his only job herding, him not wanting to side or even count.

I know you got convicts on the run and illegal aliens, but loonies? asks the sheriff.

Ernie says, I give her things to do and she does them.

She's out of her mind, sheriff, says the mother who is cooing to the baby, who is now silent, surprised at the noise the mother is making.

I may be out of my mind, I say, but I got eyes.

It looks like we are about to pull hair the next thing as the mother is taking her glasses off.

The children put down their pencil-swords and stare.

Ladies, ladies, says the sheriff. Does anyone else here know about someone missing? You all watched us count.

The people who have not left, look at each other as if they are counting and then are counting past, because they will not and never will count for someone with this blinking that he doesn't turn off, with those stars on his front and his way of speaking.

Ernie answers for them, Most everyone here minds their own business.

Now I stick my tongue out at Ernie.

McGuire, the sheriff says as quick as the tongue goes dry and gets pulled back in, Let's not waste any more of the taxpayers' money.

The two policemen open their doors and then close them, and then the machine that shrieks with the blinking comes on, accidentally, as the sheriff finds reverse and begins backing.

The shrieking is still going on when the car turns out onto the highway and one of the bigger boys, Collin in fact, breaks his pencil over his knee. But the shrieking is cut off by the time all the children start breaking theirs together and the sound of their wood-snapping runs court-wide, runs all the way out onto the highway where the sheriff leans forward to check his rear-view.

11

THIS TONGUES-OUT BUSINESS is no good, says Ernie into the darkness that lets people say what they think they think.

I am sitting on my folding chair beside my card table and Ernie is hanging around, he is coiling rope he found kids had stretched out to trip him.

It is, I say. I am not part of the world when I think I am right. That's the problem of so many years outside it and right.

Weren't you put in a place because of how you act?

I pull my holey sweater down over my sundress so it stays put at my waist, so it means business. A lot of stars on a night like tonight, I say. It's time for them to fall about now, there are too many.

Ernie arches his head back to lean over to where he can see.

I need my glasses, he says. They look like numbers in a phone book.

You are not old enough for glasses. Not that kind.

Yes, I am, says Ernie. You are just saying that to make me feel good.

Ha, I laugh. Why would I want you to feel good?

He coils his rope. Anyway, these kids, the young ones, they are the ones to stick out their tongues.

Hold my hand, I say.

He has a moment of shock, then he takes his four steps over to me, drops the rope he has been dragging and bends over to take my hand. The way he holds it it could be more rope.

See, my hands are older than the rest of me, I say. See how heavy this one is?

It is heavy, he says, and holds out his own, the free one, weighing between them. It's not that heavy.

What the hand does is nothing compared to the tongue, I say. A wild tongue, I say, is what no one forgives.

What is it? asks Ernie. What happened?

His hand, the one that holds mine, doesn't want to know. It goes here and there and he says Mmmm and Uh-huh. I tell him about my little girls anyway, how they are named

Sister and Lucy and are grown now, if they are grown. He likes that telling, it reminds him of girls, what he is after. He puts his tongue into my mouth where he says I should keep it, and he is putting the rest of himself especially close to me, so close I can feel the start of him, the very roots sprouting off his face and his tongue as a root, and all the rest.

Now this all happens quick, the time it takes to think about the last man with the Indian chanting, about that sadness I had after, and then of how a home is what Ernie has made for me here, even if he has forgotten us together in one. But it's better he doesn't remember or he might think how my doing something pulled us apart.

His hand is on me now and we are heaving toward the door in a sort of dance I've seen bees do backward, then the door is open and there is my dark floor with its nest of covers, its clothes and its found whatnots, matchbooks and toothpicks and beautiful wisps in balls that dust makes if you leave it, and I must choose now or not. This is when this choosing always happens, and this time I float away.

It's like rubber boots: when they are on, you can go through rain and choose or not to feel it. What I feel now is his skin, thick and warm across his middle where you could hide, despite his stiff shirt.

We are brother and sister, I say to him while his shirt is being lifted out.

He starts back with a breath. His what-he-has went right inside when I said brother. You are just saying that.

I put my two hands where they go on his shoulders. You tell me about that cat.

But Ernie shakes and sighs and that is that. Only when his shirt is getting tucked does he say, That cat? Look, I tell everybody I am this person. I just go along every day without that person who you say knows a cat story. I go along like someone who has just dropped in, Hi, everybody. All I am saying is that I remember what I can.

Oh, I say.

All I am saying, I say after we are outside and Ernie is back with his rope, all I am saying is that you can't always cut out the tongue.

What about your husband? asks Ernie. He frames my eye in a loop of rope. Don't you have one?

I practiced, like they say about lawyers and doctors. I don't say Yes. I say they're both dead and tall. Not like you.

Don't tell me, says Ernie. Don't tell me now. He knots the rope.

It's never all told, I say. It's never now.

Ollie, ollie, oxen free, cries one of the children from somewhere not far away. A TV roars like an answer, then gets quieted.

I ask, Do you remember the Santa with the rubber band birds? The ones that flew out of the envelopes and hurt us?

Other kids went home to presents and Santas and all we had from that Santa that they took us to was a practical joke, a whir and a whack, and later our pretend home to go to, with presents that had our last names first tagged on, like they got them from out of a long line in the alphabet.

I don't remember none of it.

Some days when I was still small, I say, playing with the cat that has shown up for the rope, I wanted to ink up my finger and press it across the moon so you could see my print from wherever you were. The print is the only part that is real, that can't be changed or lied about.

Now there is a bad idea. Ernie looks up at what moon is left. Already somebody screwed it up from the looks of it to me. See all that grey part?

That's your eyes, I say, and laugh. That smear part—that's your bad eyes.

It doesn't matter, I can't see it, he says. It doesn't matter, that's all. Don't tease.

You can't see it like you can't see the girl in the gully, I say. Then I say, Quiet.

Whatever else is not quiet, is scratching.

Hear it? I ask.

Bugs, he says, big bugs.

He is lifting one foot and then the other, but he is not stepping on them because the sound is not there and not like that. Go on, he says. You don't hear a girl. You don't even hear me. You make me short and foolish and young when I'm none of that. I was the second tallest from the fifth grade, nobody but one girl was taller.

Me, I say. I was the one girl taller.

He drags his circles of rope away from me so the dust, white light, follows him, and the grass he passes over flattens in that end-of-season way which is permanent. He shouts after himself, You're from across the state. You didn't go to this fifth grade.

I wasn't always put away, I yell. You think people get born there? I moved around, I moved around with you. Once.

I been a lot of places, he says. He is hardly talking loud enough for me now because he is spooking away so fast. I see his rope making its way in between two trailers that look hunched they are that tipped, and the cat behind it.

I stay out longer. No one else comes out since prime time is on and even the smallest kids are inside for their dose of men with guns and breasted women. I have had all of that onscreen stuff and nothing more and no choice for so long that I'm not letting its screams lure me back, I'm not pulling my chair over to where a set is, where the high notes run out with hate. Let there be live opera like on the channel you pay for, only real, women singing like nobody wants them to shut up, those screams.

12

I THOUGHT I GREW UP IN homes but really I grew up after, in the places that I was checked into. In the homes I had to look after myself and sometimes parents too so it was hard to have time to grow up. In this place that was for the not-quite-right, the places for the listing left or right, I was not supposed to look after anyone, just to set and be, which makes you crazy enough to figure out how not to want anyone to look after you ever, and to grow up.

It was a mistake I went in to begin with, like when they arrest you for joking about the kid squirt gun you have locked in your luggage. It was just after I had the number two baby and we made up a whole family, two girls and me, a home. I didn't leave them alone a minute, I tell you, I couldn't leave them alone—no, never, we would stay together and eat every day together, we would love. Never mind the man with the slight huskiness who was good for a war dance or a dance for rain but was not one to be with. He was so soon gone I was still sitting in my nightgown with a wet front because of all the milk, and worse, the tears I made remembering what he was good for in that short time. But someone was sitting there listening to me remember. After a while I said to that someone, I see frogs in the wall, and I didn't have a fever. That someone asked me to choose—Did I or did I not see frogs? And I chose. Painters see frogs and even people in walls and all they do is just fill them in, why should it matter with me just because I don't fill them in? And just because a painter is silent, filling them in, doesn't mean he can't talk about them or even with them if he wants to. There I was with just all this talk about frogs. Talk like that does not make me someone who should not stay together with her babies and her home, it makes me someone with words.

That someone thought she was doing the greater good, two babies' good against mine. In fact it was the three of us doing the good together. But soon the two had homes. I know this because the fathers weren't ones to keep them, if they could even be found. But where the girls' homes were no one would tell me. Once one of the parents of the homes made them visit, but by then I could see they didn't see me, they saw where I was and they didn't come again. They went home.

I see their tied-in-the-back bows now as they left, bows fluffed out by someone into bow-presents, into fancy monkey bottoms or a great set of fish fins.

I am walking on the ocean again. The gully has its wave chop frozen in great rises of dirt so I can walk into its bottom and wait for the pretend water to crash down with the fish. Brown fish mostly, but in some lights they'd be mauve, that word they use for clothes or lipstick that's hard to sell. Nothing does crash down, of course, but I have to watch my way or I will lose it, I will drown in these brown waves.

Today I find a dugout. Snakes and dogs have holes here, maybe even the cats I have heard of. This hole is big though, and goes in sideways, with earth over it. A piece of glass is what showed it to me, glass in the side of its brown wave like an eye that could be window. Otherwise, the dugout's hardly a stop in the ocean with its no road in front, not even a breath's hesitation between one wave going over another that would say here is where you could dream a drowning.

I walk over to it. Flowers that no one planted still spurt out of the roof although it is late, it is cool now, but their dead dry spray makes it cheerful on top so I'm not afraid of it. The inside is, however, like any hole, dark, and no one or nothing is in it, but someone could be, it is that big. And there is something inside, a scratched-on pot so black it's nearly all shadow, and a line of twigs that don't come from here because here is a no-trees place. There's ash too, a lot of the smell of ash.

A dugout like in the picture in the institution I would not look at because it was no comfort.

I sit down.

The ocean is what I see sitting down and watching out the hole. This land that is ocean is held together by birds who rise and dip and sew all the waves together and when they fall flat down into it, dead, their bones, especially the petrified ones, show all the stitches.

Plenty of rabbits cross here too. I'm sure of it. Rabbits mean the country's useless and gone wrong. All these hopping, helpless rabbits with just speed on their side and fur the color of the waves without anything or anyone to check and balance them, wolves for instance, mean that.

So a girl could live here. I hear a rattling and get out of there, but she could hear it too and live. She would not be caught like a cow with only the whites of her eyes showing, caught completely in snow or mud or the back end of a fence or with a snake. She is not lost the way I thought. She's in the hole.

Maybe in the hole. I march rock over to where it is, scrub rocks that hardly hold up when they're moved. They could be white cowchips with let-go like that. I move the rocks into a line so you can see that this is the place. Then I worry this is touching the nest so the bird won't return and I move all the rocks back and I try to remember it without the rocks, walking backward for a while, watching the way I would go to find it.

The sun on my back shows that frost has already laid itself down here because the bunch grass is red, the color that people think I mean when I say, Look, look at the red. Well, it is red enough. What I say also is, Is that cow red? Would you call that red? And they always say, Well, no. It's not really red but red-brown. Not red the way the black cows are black. See, I say.

I walk around a big skull I find out in the middle of the gully. I know children come here. The skull is lifted out of the ground and the teeth are taken out by someone needing teeth for a game, and then the skull is left looking at the court which is too far away to be seen from here. I touch where those eyes would turn, I make them turn.

She's nowhere in them, though. Not learning her A, B, C's. No. Singing about spiders? No. Or *Rockabye*, that song that the baby comes crashing down in? No. She is where someone with special eyes would find her if they could.

The sun waffles against the waves and lets the dark in.

I touch the ruined teeth of the pocket barrette.

What she needs is someone to protect her, a Kate, so in a home when they lay blame, she is there, the one who asks first for another cover and gets the No. That is why I had two, why two is all you need.

Why does Kate leave her there?

To protect the others.

What from?

The lights are turned on for me so far away. Come on home they twinkle in a code I can read without knowing Morse or any of the shorthand signals or anything about spies.

13

PLEASE STOP SHUSH-SHUSHING those big feet of yours like we are lined up to the graveyard and go, says Ernie to the mechanic.

Ernie is in the front position of the slick plastic-shrouded couch and the mechanic is in a babystep behind, the couch being so long it looks like it stretches even longer each step. Let's go, says Ernie.

Good works take time, says the mechanic, step by slow step. He is, after all, blind, and when he heard the sound of a dropoff—the clunk of couch off the back end of the van it came on—he shuffled over and offered himself up to help. Such a couch with four matching plaid foam-filled pillows is full work for two men since it certainly will not bend around the corners of the several trailers that block its way. Besides, Ernie did sell nearly every single chance that he had printed up to benefit the mechanic's new glasses, though they are not yet bought or even measured for.

At last the mechanic lowers his end into place, the sit-down spot under Ernie's big window.

Like rats to a ship, kids show at the site, swarm the vinyl as it is heaved into another final position by Ernie's foot and then heaved again to get it off a bump, and then again.

This is brand new, says Ernie to the kids as if this is not why they are there. Get off it.

Ernie waves his hands and tries to adjust for the bump and get them away at the same time. People start to appear, caught by the noise of the swarm which is louder than their sets.

Ernie shakes his head at the children who do not budge, then at the gathering adults, saying again and with his hands, Get them off of here. He gives up, touches the shoulder of the mechanic who today is wearing his commando beret from the *theater*, the place he served and returned from without an audience which he is fond of pointing out often to any and all, and especially to those who want him to assist in their mechanical repairs despite his blindness, and Ernie says I do thank you.

The mechanic pulls the beret forward and off his head. I would give you the time of day, he says. I would change your tire. He replaces the beret, more or less.

Several of the kids put their hands on their chests and mumble about their tires, with giggles.

Hmmm, says Ernie. He pulls out a wad of tickets. Take yourself a few of these chances from this other shop, he says. Why, who knows? You might win big like me. They got a bedroom set on this one.

He presses a select group into the mechanic's hand, batting away the kids who grope, who buzz around. The tickets won't bite. No, they won't, he says. Just be sure to keep track of the date—it might be coming up real soon. Get someone to check for you.

The mechanic closes his hand just in time for the jostling of kids back onto the couch and the wildness they raise, flipping themselves over it onto the vinyl slap of the seat and back again.

Go on, get. Ernie reaches for his aerial, now bent but still unbroken. He waves it.

The children do go then, they do scatter a few feet.

Ernie takes his seat on the couch which still rocks a touch.

What a whale! exclaims a someone.

Put a motor on it, says another someone.

I think you got the turkey this time, says someone else.

Go on, says Ernie. Go on or I'll raise your lot fee a quarter, he says, rearing up off the couch in a huff.

Someone hears a phone ring and someone has to cover their cactus collection. They go, steering the mechanic home and shaking their heads, and they barely have the mechanic's shuffling started when the kids begin to swarm again.

Ernie whips his aerial around his head as if it is a lasso, but the kids swear they are already bored. Then they all leave the couch with a hesitation that says they'll be back as quick as he is turned.

Wait a minute, he says. Don't you go, little lady. Come on over here. Yes, you.

I avoid his grab. I am one of the ones who saw the size of this couch and followed it in wonderment.

I got a place to sit now, he says, in his own style of sweet talk.

I see that, I say. What are you going to do when the weather changes?

Ernie turns to examine the couch length seriously, in particular the three feet that bob past the end of the trailer, or what he calls his office, the word to go with the sign overhead carved out in *Manager.*

I'm going to build me some overhang, he says, that's what I'm going to do. He slaps at the trailer metal like it is a girl's skin, then turns to me, pulling a face as if this is too much to ever consider, this hide-away attachment and the problem of the bump so why ask? He sinks his sinking eyes on me but what he sees in my front snaps him out of it, helps him forget his problem and its sometime solution, and he says, You're going to sit with me on this couch, yes you are. Every time you finish picking the fence like I told you, you are going to come and sit. It is a kind of reward.

I got my own place to sit, I say, and I take a step back toward that place.

You sit right down here in my goddamn just-won couch, goddammit. Ernie is crossing his arms now, he is mad. Sit and talk the way we did in the home.

The home? I say. Now you remember the home?

Someplace that started with an G.

Gregg. We used to sit on their couch in the dark, I say. It wasn't always at the table, with food in front of us that was bad, and your cat stories.

I knew there was a couch. But I was not there for long. A new home, pronto, if you please, he says, with pretend cheer, rubbing his hands together as if that would get them clean.

Yes, there was a new home, I say. Do you remember why we both got new homes, one for me and one for you, separate?

Ernie is standing by my side now but petting the couch's

vinyl. Sit down, he says instead of answering. What's wrong with my couch to sit on?

Nothing, I say. But this is how it is: I got too many homes not to want my own chair. I sit on my own chair in front of my own place, thank you, I say. Even if you remember that home, I sit on my own chair.

Your chair? Ernie spits.

He walks clear across the court to my folding chair, he picks it up, he carries it over to his couch, he sets the chair right down next to it.

I cross my arms.

Sit, he says.

Please, he says.

I lift my chin into the air, then I take the chair with one hand and move it an inch away from the couch. I'm sitting, I say, and I am.

Ernie scowls a little smile. I am, after all, sitting nearby. He sits on the spot of couch closest to me. See how it's all waves from the wind, he says, plunging right into the talking, pointing down into the empty gully.

I thought that already, I say. How the wind will push the waves of land that way until the end of the world.

The wind is pretty tough. See all the soapweed too, to go with the chop? he says. You could have a bath.

He laughs for me. He makes the couch rock on the bump

as if it is a rocking couch. I found a petrified snail out there in it, he says, fooling with the leg.

There are fish too in those waves, I say, putting my arm up over the folding chair back. The Lord will have to let us know when that flood is coming.

Two by two then, says Ernie.

I don't know about that, I say, and I'm looking at him sideways. That is so dull.

Really? says Ernie. Two by two? He is inching toward me.

I tell him I would go into solitary for that kind of talk, the soap-in-the-mouth kind. Which only makes me think about it more, I say. Two by two! I am giggling now, uncontrollably, my arms thrown in front of me, my head bowed.

Ernie moves all the way down his too big couch away from me.

It is not big enough.

14

SMALL, QUICK AND DIRTY HANDS play with the cup, prop it up on a clod of the gully's limestone, pick it up after it tumbles. Then there's a knee with a scab righting the cup from the other side, a finger nudging a twig on top across the cup, then the back of a head with its hair, followed by the flank of a cow. When that's past, the cow lowing and lumbering, the child and the cup are both gone, the limestone's smashed by the cow's walk, and a fine cloud from its smashing drifts off gully-side into dusk.

Another fine cloud runs its way opposite, car dust from a long car coming.

15

A BUCKET OF WATER HOLDS itself at a teeter on top until the two boys slam the door in their wild chasing. Then the bucketful wets them from top to bottom, and the two, with guns full of the same, twirl their now all-wet selves in a way that shows they don't miss the late real gun-thick programs, and they fire, water up and out, wetting everywhere water will carry.

And with a lot of surprise—nothing is worse than getting wet without warning, the two boys say with their wild squirting.

From a step or two behind the door, Kate hooks the fallen water bucket handle with some old lady's cast-off cane broken by a semi backing a trailer down their entry road, the road now filled with a station wagon going forward. Kate notices the car as she gets the bucket, as she runs to the tap and refills it in the squirting wildness of getting even, the water rushing loud as it does from an outdoor tap into a bucket. But it is then that Freddie finds her, then that she grabs up the cane and topples his bucket again, the wake wetting the boy's shoes worse but mostly allowing her getaway.

Freddie is quick with a gun. He soon has her backed into the plug side of the electronic pinball, squirting and squirting, and he's giggling in spite of himself, though she's shrieking a fair defense.

Kate! Kate! That is her mother's call, shrill but not far away, not far enough away. I am bringing water for my saucepan from the squirted-up washroom and I don't miss the flinch and dart in Kate's eyes.

Kate kicks the empty bucket into Freddie to show she can hear, but not kicking at full force or mean, and he keeps on squirting but not as much or in places that can hurt.

Kate!

There's dusk mixed up in this that lets Kate stall.

Oh, get going, says Freddie, at last closer to Kate and seeing her shiver.

This time Kate kicks the bucket into his knees just to do it. Or because it is pity she hates even if it is good for her. Then Collin's coming around the corner, gun weeping at the seams it is so full, and her mother is already pitching her Kate! like she knows just where Kate is, so Kate tears off over that fallen bucket.

I am now in the way with my saucepan, which swishes its water over the top onto her when she bumps into it or my elbow, but what's in the saucepan hardly wets her more, she is so soaked. Kate! and Beat you! are the three words which hurry her, not so much the boys with their guns or the water from the pan.

At my trailer I drop two dogs into my saucepan water.

The dusk hides where exactly Kate gets her wallop. When she cries, Collin did it and not Freddie, Freddie is farther than ever from her, and it is the sound of anger in a flat board that is heard being aimed at her.

I boil the dogs in the silence after such a whacking, when kids keep so quiet with all the squirting gone out of them. I won't! is the last Kate says in the high scream of beaten pain, then the slam comes from the door which is not much of a slam, those doors on trailers catching instead, but enough for me to drop the hot dog fishing it out and then have to find it all over again with my fingers.

I coat the dog with ketchup, then I take a big bite, then I chew, then I stop and listen.

The boys have turned their guns on each other, long sprays in the twilight that speak more of their range than of where the water lands, and the pursuit is now silent. Children caught in the crossfire don't squeal much but watch the two of them fire and flee.

All the other adults sit inside with their shows, with their news and ads for news.

I stop watching and listen, I take a sip from my mug of hot dog water.

The children run toward the entry, their guns dry, at least the two boys', and there they go on playing under the single streetlight beside the long car that is parked there.

I am listening, I don't take another bite.

Perhaps something rattles.

I lean forward and in leaning, deposit the rest of the dog back onto my paper plate, which must have been washed three times by now, the nap of it is so rough and ditched. I lick the ketchup off my finger and listen.

There's a bug noise, a little of that. What else?

I look all around, even shift my bum to get the far side view, then I decide to ease onto my knees and peer under my trailer.

It's dark, fully dark.

I rise and brush my knees clean, fish out the other dog, and place it alongside the half-eaten one, then tuck the plate under the trailer, into the dark of that one-foot space.

A cat as dark as that space inches forward.

Shoo, I say with my hands. The cat snarls in a wild way but I shoo it again. It doesn't leave but chooses to spit at me.

I flap my arms. Shoo. I take out the dogs and pour ketchup on the bare one. Cats don't go for ketchup like girls. I shove both dressed dogs under again and the cat rears back in her No. But when it finally does pad off, all of whatever else is gone too.

I take back my seat and sip my drink, all I have left now.

Daddy! cries Kate from the eclipse of the cracked-open doorjoint not far off. My little girl, he says as he slips in through it. Then an ashtray is thrown, not a book I decide since the mechanic's nailed down Bible is the only book I've ever seen in the court, and a thud like an ashtray hits something not too hard yet something with bulk.

Everything goes quiet then.

I tuft my sweater, find the few balls of fluff that haven't yet formed. I'm not looking at where all the trailer trouble is, but I have ears. Trouble always has its noise.

It's a champion quiet.

I retrieve my worn plate from underneath. It's empty enough, the nap clean of ketchup.

I smile all the way to my shoulders. Still on my knees, I see her red. I make cat scratch sounds and back away.

16

People think people who live in these places are just caught here but for some, like Ernie, trailer life is the same as teepee life and those are people who know all about the land, they talk to one another about who first and what next and why—they chant about it. It is home to them, a home people want just as bad as any other, a home with a history a person could know and tell.

What I know from Ernie is this place was not so empty a hundred years before. Wagons, the first trailers, were parked within sight of each other but not too close because within sight meant you got only what land was in between. Then crops were sown in between, and every pass of the plough kept hold of the land, whether anything grew or not.

People put up first in the places where the wagons trailed past, to see and call out to the next wagons about their belongings, about wives lost or never come, or broken axles that never did work and were reordered and where were they? After a while, all that frontage was taken, back to back, and those who came second got seconds, got even gully land that should never have been turned, where only the long-toothed animals should have gnawed, not sheep or goats ever. Plenty of second settlers actually settled deep in the seconds of the gully, too tired or broke or stubborn to go on. Ernie's grandfather was all of that, but he had Ernie's belief in luck. That's what Ernie says.

I heard this gully had luck for a while when it had a climate to speak of. That's all luck is with a place, the right climate and enough word-of-mouth to suck farmers and even sailors across continents full of land and the many oceans adjacent. People are fascinated by luck, but best by bad luck because if it's not theirs it could be, it could be coming and to them, whereas good luck is more like lightning, something that refuses to take turns. Ernie is having his turn now and considers it good, this court he's got from his grandfather, and his mother who, he says, starved he sucked on her so much. He did have to wait for his luck however, he had to wait until he came of age after all those years of homes.

Ernie's lucky now—see that couch?

I stand next to it, telling him if he is the court, I am the empty gully. Ernie is quick to say all he got was his grandfather's dugout though it was, he admits, zoned for a court, but his trailer doesn't sit right because of that dugout, let alone the couch. I stand back and see it does rise a little over all the others, lifted like something someone could envy, land-lust after, and not even know why.

The sun sinks into the gully dip first, giving the court that much more sun, making it shine against its dark the way the face of the mother who says the carpet sweeper handle whacked her, who shows the dead canary woman how the handle came up and blackened her eye and not an ash tray, who shows her, patient as a friend.

The long car with *Lyle's Locks* on it is gone.

17

FALL IS FALLING FAST, FASTER every night. The kids have barely torn up their school papers when there's darkness in the air of the smoke those papers turn into, flaring with their matchbook lightings. I'm waving one of my old plates, now about as thin as tissue, over a little flame eating those leftover trash papers and a few others, wish scraps, the torn-out pictures of dolls and bikes and blocks that will never be seen on trailer grounds. I let these wish scraps pile up in case they need to be peeled off the fence to get put back in a pocket or under a pillow. Some do. It's the all-grey ones that get burned.

I toss in my plate too. The wind, always cheerful when it comes to fire, pinwheels a few gusts so the plate soon catches and flares. I stomp out all its red and the embers go wild, crazy as fireflies, spinning in the updraft that the gully pulls down into the dark.

But the embers light nothing.

I return to my trailer and set up dinner: a new plate for dogs, three of them boiling away on the burner with its red eye that sparks now and then from dust that sticks to the filaments. I fork the dogs out and set them down.

I have already bitten the back end off the first one and am chewing when I shove the second under the trailer on the plate. When I get up off my knees, my dead canary neighbor is behind me.

What are you feeding? she asks me. I didn't see you come in with a pet. You're not allowed a pet unless it's an approved pet.

Instead of the bird, she now has a daschund that she uses the nose of to gesture with, a daschund she keeps locked in her forearm.

It's just food for wild things, I say. You know—those that don't get fed every day with catfood and whatever. I block her possible view of the food.

The neighbor shifts her large weight and the dog and tries to see around me. That's going to attract a lot worse than cats, she says and points approximately. Honest to god, one time I had a wildcat spray my sidewalls until the paint peeled. Like Bozo the Clown, that cat was, fur sticking out of both sides of his chops. Why, soon I was afraid he'd come in and get the leftovers himself. I fed a dog inside for a year after that, with those wet pellets that stink up the place so bad.

I hike up my slip, a complicated fumble with my good number of straps. Those kinds of cats, I say, aren't really so wild. They are out there because they have no place else.

No. They are another kind of cat, they don't belong in homes. They are really wild.

I'd like to see one like that. You think they're out here?

Well, no. Or could be. I mean I haven't seen one for a long while now and none of the calves have been taken for quite some time. Used to be every spring they'd find a cat of that kind curled up inside the hollowed out stomach of a cow. Cats like that could still be around.

Could be? I say and I look behind the neighbor like I am catching sight of one, or enough so that the woman takes her eyes off the underneath part where I put the plate. Then the daschund sneezes and takes an interest in her armpit and whines. The neighbor shushes it by squeezing but instead of squeaking like a toy, the dog goes limp and quiet, but not dead limp.

You know I don't think you're taking me too seriously, she

says. Next thing, critters will be coming in through your trailer exhaust—and mine too.

I believe it, I say and nod.

You'd better believe it, says the neighbor, turning heavily, dog ass-out. You could get yourself in trouble.

As soon as the woman gets hold of the stair rail to her aluminum steps, I pick up my last dog and aim it at her.

Bang! The dog goes off. But only in my head. I'm getting careful now with my tongue, more careful than a canary with the gas left on, I hope.

18

KATE'S SLIGHTLY ROUNDED chest, with its brown circles, nipples but no real swell, heaves under her hair where a brush scours that nipple and leaves a faint scratch as it tries to match the hair to the shine of the grape barrette that catches it, the barrette that gets yanked out.

I am putting numbers on my mailbox in case I get mail—no one can put on names, they change too much for Ernie to allow it—and I am as still as a deer beside my box. Their back window is open enough that I can see in their mirror that the mother is covering the scratch and an unblinking Kate with a tattered slip, with a new party dress.

You can cry if you want to, sings her mother, fastening that barrette a second time, this time a little higher and tighter, so you can see the girl feels her eye socket skin stretching.

It's not my party, says Kate. It's not any party, she says. Her shoulders make a slight shake.

We don't want Daddy to go away again, says her mother. All you have to do is sing—that's what he said. You remember the words?

Que sera, sera, says Kate.

Her mother is doing her own hair now, brushing it up over her head in a fountain in the mirror. Her eyes don't find me or follow her daughter's. Her eyes, in fact, can't follow. She does keep singing, however. *If it happens to you,* she sings.

I have to calm him down, her mother says. I can't bother with you children when he comes. You just help calm him down.

I don't like to, says Kate.

The mother turns from the mirror. Why do you get the dresses and not me? she asks.

Kate looks at her shoulder.

You be good to him, says the mother.

The mother wags her head like a girl on a merry-go-round, so clever in the way she does it. Maybe she thinks she is on a merry-go-round and we're all watching her in the mirror, her smeared red lips, her glasses on crooked.

The mother does say she is dizzy and takes a drag on a cigarette.

Kate's face is closed to the dizziness. All she sees is her mother removing a long vial from under the sink. Which isn't for you, says the mother. No, it's not. And the mother smiles at it, not the daughter. Come here, she says. I need your sash.

There's the bang of a hairbrush hitting the door.

Kate is out. She runs straight past me and my mailbox and right down into the gully, the two long sashes streaking out behind her, sashes that can be pulled back like reins for a game of dogtrot or crossed in front like the Virgin Mary, or even circled around an arm and pulled tight to make what the needle wants.

The mother doesn't go to the door, however. She doesn't see the dress tear on the fence when Kate climbs it or how the other children have to track Kate down into the dusty white rocked gully. The mother checks back in the mirror instead, to see if it still shows her fountaining hair, her red lips, her long arm, and the stuck-up needle.

19

A SINGLE SPARKLER FLARES and sputters out.

Freddie's master of the matches but Collin has hold of the unlit rest and between the two of them it is a struggle to get them lit at all. They both have burns. But they are not quarreling or the others would quickly take over. How long did you have them in your drawer? is all Freddie asks me, to show everything's fine, everything will get lit.

She's the trash lady, says Collin, she found them in the trash. He's pulling the sparkler a little away from Freddie so it's hard to light, so Freddie has to move.

I back up fast. Freddie's sparkler shoots out suddenly. Collin quick lights the rest in his hand from Freddie's as if he has planned it that way. The other children dive to arm themselves, to race in circles with the sparklers, to zigzag and hide and try to touch the tips to each other.

Spell her name! shouts Collin over their yells.

Lay off, Freddie shouts back.

You like her, says Collin, coming closer.

Go to hell, says Freddie, backing off.

Spell it out loud, says Collin and jabs his sparkler at Freddie's neck.

K-A-, says Freddie, moving his in front of Collin's eyes, very close to Collin's eyes.

Cut it out, says Collin, then Freddie does, all at once.

What's that? he says.

What's what? shrieks a girl who steals her light from his sparkler now fast going out.

See? Beyond his pointing hand is a match just then struck way off at the edge of the court. And another one.

What? asks Collin. I don't see. What?

The lights are gone.

Made you look, says Freddie, spinning his sparkler stub.

Did not, says Collin, his dying out.

Did too, says Freddie.

All the sparklers sputter out at once.

I go inside for a blanket and the rest of what I can find in my drawer. The kids all bunch up around me as soon as I come out. I've got the box broken open and a dozen hands are at me when a man's voice shouts out of the dark, You get on home right this minute.

No way, all the children yell back. They charge that dark, screaming and hiding in the corners that trailers and trailer parts make. To taunt, they clang on the broken swingset with the sparkler wires and then clang the propane tanks rowed like spaceship air. None of them want to hear whatever that voice says about home in that dark so they stick to that dark, they pull it over their heads and wear it. But into those hardly ever used corners they hide in creeps TV light, especially during the commercials—and that's what the man sees with, this big man with his not-old looks and no flowers.

Get home! he barks into that light. He is drunk and shuffling or he would easily hear what comes next. Sometimes a child can't hold back fear and sound tears out of his mouth and the child starts, hearing it, wondering how a sound like that could happen, and ends up making two sounds.

The second time the man hears Collin and grabs him.

Where's your sister? he says rough, like the boy is hiding her behind him. He crouches all his large self down to the boy's height. Or else, he says into his face, and twists his arm.

Kate walks out then.

Let's see that new dress, he orders, still holding Collin too tight. You like it? he says, pushing her into the TV light.

The dress is twisted and smudged and torn but Kate

doesn't say sorry or why, doesn't even look up at him or at Collin. Her eyes look elsewhere. She is elsewhere, the child who has begun to shake isn't Kate.

He doesn't notice the shaking or the dress tears in this dark. He is too drunk, leaning over, asking her again, louder, You like it? when sparklers explode from the catty-corner darkness, one big bunch especially which comes right at the man and his open mouth.

Daddy! says Collin.

The man whacks the lit ones away so the burning wires fall on Collin and the children and they scream as the sparklers spray at them and their eyes, their mouths, their skin.

A last one he kicks at and stomps out.

Come on, he says. Now. He grabs Kate's arm and tightens his hand on Collin's and drags the two of them backwards over the bumpy ruts that cars go on. Goddamn kids, he says.

The man doesn't hear someone sneaking around, he drags the two kids a good ten feet and then says, You run along now and tell your mother to heat up the soup. But drunk, it comes out, Beat up the stoop. Beat it up, he says. I'll fix your britches, he hisses to the child that is left, the one he doesn't let go, who can't run off with the message of stoop, or slip back to be with the children who are still out, who haven't been called, who won't go in.

Kate runs home.

Someone is sneaking around while the man starts whistling cheerfully, a whistle then stop, whistle then stop. Someone sneaks around the length of two trailers in the whistling silence when all of a sudden there's more light, a lot more—electricity at the end of a snaky and wild homemade cable and a bang, a blow-up pop of light that makes it day, the blinded color of an eyeball.

But I'm not blind. Pink is what I see. A wet pink, a worked down suit and the man puckered up to whistle. But that's not all, a bit of a boy flattened, his pants down too.

The man sees me, I see him.

My TV! yells someone. My TV, someone moans.

Doors open, slam. What's the big idea? someone says. What's the big, fucking idea.

Light flashes, light spouts from the end of the cable.

It's the end, yells the mechanic who must see something. Get the gooks! He runs out of his trailer, holding a grease gun half the length of it.

The electricity's in spasms now, making the cable bend and arc up, in no direction but frantic: out, out, out. The tail of light whips six ways more, but I don't see the man and the boy and what they are doing again.

She's who did it, says the man with the scar across his face like a pumpkin's, who sees me from the side of a flash, who points at me pressed up against my table. He says this as if the electricity had my name on it instead of his, as if the cables weren't slithering off his homemade box. She's the one with the rake who did it, he says.

More electricity gets loosed in roars. People scream but I've had electricity, I can take it.

Ernie hustles over, his shoes off, his shower thongs slapping.

Light behind the pumpkin-faced man makes his skin red along the scar line. What he accuses me of I can't hear, the sound flies right off him and goes elsewhere because of the electrical noise and of me not listening, me seeing the man moving toward me, the boy in the grip of his hand.

Thanks, I hear my daschund- and dead-canary-loving neighbor say to me. Thanks a lot.

It's not her, says the man when he reaches the crowd. I think just the cable broke, he says. The man nods his head as if he has the only answer, but I know the nod is meant to say, Shut up, and that the nod is for me.

Hey, the phones are dead, someone shouts.

You—Lyle, says Ernie. You can pull that car out of the drive and get us some help.

The man walks to his car, still holding the boy's hand. After he seatbelts the boy in, he says, Stay away until the police come. Ernie, you tell them. And keep those kids out of it.

Keep those kids away, echoes Ernie, who has found his aerial and is using it.

Then the man is gone and so is all the power. It whines, it wiggles, then it goes off of its own accord. Maybe that is all the power it had, it was a well that had just run dry.

The dark is now really dark. Only the mechanic can see and help us, can feel for the trailer panels as he fumbles for doors and their catches, his grease gun cocked and in the way and him talking in some other language, maybe what he heard in his war.

Does anyone have candles? everyone asks everyone. This is not a place big on staying prepared. Someone has a votive which someone else cuts in half. Flashlights flash and wane and get checked for batteries, shook up and looked into. Someone says, Girls who are afraid of the dark can sleep with me. And someone says, They're going to make us pay. That trash lady, someone else says, and it is the man with the pumpkin scar.

By the time I am back inside and the held breath I get when I hear myself being made part of a problem escapes, a stink drifts in where the thinnest electrical smoke drifts skyward, marking where the tail of power had twisted, so reluctant now to let any out at all. It is a hell smoke, I decide, the poof! that made this photo in my head of a father and son, a flash on a thought I almost can't have.

20

THE WIND IS ALL OVER everywhere the next day. All that snap and frolic the black cable made the night before—that's just a crackle in the wind now—and the power people who are here to put it under wraps have the power up but not fixed all over, no, not fixed until someone pays up. Their job is just to give power to the ones who were hooked up the way they were supposed to be, the good ones, but slowly, a little power at a time.

It's just the wind that's wild now, so wild McGuire has a hard time tying the Police Line tape around the stakes that the power company has already sectioned off the trailer with, the one that sucked in all that homemade power, the pumpkin-faced man's who owes the most. McGuire has to put his tape around it too because the sheriff is repossessing for all of the money owed but it is hard for McGuire to do this wrapping, not because his heart is soft and he wishes the man a better shake, but because the wind grabs at the tape ends as it flops against the stakes.

Two of the power men eat sandwiches against that trailer, two uniformed men with double-deckers and lots of time before they have to go back to work on the homemade power mess. McGuire has been quite good at circling the stakes with tape so the uniformed men who watch know he is a man who can do at least this part well, yes, the tape comes out of his pocket smooth as a tape for measuring but now he has to fasten it together to stay, and the knot he makes turns in on itself and won't stay, and each time the wind knows that.

He goes back to his patrol car for what? He has no stapler, nothing else to join the ends. In the emergency kit the best he finds is string. With string you ought to be able to do something, he decides, and he balls it up in his hand.

Such a big important man with such a problem, says someone as McGuire exits the car, ass-first since he was just leaning in.

The man talking is just standing there.

What? asks McGuire, banging his head on the door frame to catch what he thinks he hears, the man so close so suddenly.

Why do you do it, McGuire? The man is just asking, that's what his voice says, nice and easy.

McGuire puts the ball of string into his pocket. Is the wind twisting what he hears? What does he hear?

Your wife is a thinker, I'll bet she thinks about you. The man goes on.

You're drunk, says McGuire. I could take you in. McGuire is looking around.

I'm not driving, says the man. I'm not on public property, he says.

You are disturbing the peace, says McGuire. You know? Don't give me a reason. He pulls on the end of the string until it hangs out of his pocket, the motion jiggling the cuffs clipped to his side.

You just keep doing what you're doing, the man says, opening his car door with his name across it.

Shut yourself up, says McGuire. He steps over and grabs the man's arm to make sure he hears, then repeats himself.

That's what I intend to do, the man says. Just don't bother me. Then everything will be all right. All right? You know?

McGuire knows how much he wants to know. He lets go of the man's arm. The man straightens up, smoothes his pretend army clothes, his not-old face.

You are disgusting, says McGuire.

Me? asks the man.

McGuire's eyes fix on the whipping tape as the man leaves.

I see all this between them and I hear it all too because I'm checking if this skinny grass to the south of my trailer is fall onion, onion that comes up and gets caught in snow if you have some, and this leaves me on my knees and very, very close to that car and its two people.

McGuire holds the tape and just holds it until finally one of the power people comes up with a staple gun and helps him fix it. He leaves quick after that, down that same long, skinny road that the man with a load of lock samples has already driven off on.

21

I THINK IT IS SO NICE WITHOUT electricity, like before this was land and just part of the earth and no one's. Or everyone's—that must be it—the stars so spread with nothing in the way and the night full of only sleep, with no one to turn the electric off and say you missed your medicine or a show. Or to give you electricity. The dark comes down hard this way but there's still the trailer's candles and high beams and of course, the stars. For dinner, those who have them find grills and sear frozen food on top of what charcoal is left after summer. For a while, the red eyes of that heat glows making the spread legs of the charcoal unit look as if they hold up a burning nose cone. Those without grills eat from cans, in the moonlight off the moon of those lids.

Tonight I am not worried about anyone seeing my line with the dog on the end of it lying under my trailer. If the line jumps, I will pull it closer. I could reel it in any time I want. But then my neighbor with the daschund lets her dog out.

My neighbor doesn't close the door right away after she lets it out. She tries to look into the dark after it. She lifts her candle which is cupped by her hand against the slight wind and I'm caught in her light.

Rat, I've got me a rat, I tell her right away. A rat we don't need in this dark.

You bet, says my neighbor, but don't you go and catch yourself a dog, my dog.

She slams the door behind her.

I wait until the scratching of her animal starts and then stops after she lets it in, and then I pull out the line and the dog there is gone too.

I eat the other dog, facing the gully. A few humps of cow that are too big for brush stand at the bottom with eyes that the stars catch on. Maybe the girl in red will come out of the gully and stay close to me now that she is less hungry. Or maybe because she is less hungry, she will stay away.

A baby cries behind me and sometimes any baby can be anyone's and I turn to fetch it, forgetting.

22

THE PINBALL MAN LEANS over his machine and doesn't ever blink. Other machines around him bang and froth, and scum makes a path to his boot, but he doesn't go over and kick at the machines or even straighten out a load. He likes the banging and the way it sometimes goes with the flow, bangs when he bangs on the glass top that's going to crack someday if he doesn't watch out but that he bangs at anyway to get the ball down.

I am trouble however. I am all around him, half inside the driers, my arm up to the elbow in a washer. At least I'm not a talker-to-myself, at least he hasn't heard me talk that way. No, I come right up and talk right to him, spoiling whatever score he's got going.

Today I have bothered him about a last cricket caught behind a washer, a cricket, as I say to him, that would make a good snack with chocolate on it. I say chocolate makes them tasty, that nobody will starve so long as there's crickets and chocolate around. He Uh-huhs his way through that one and still gets a double free game, and I can see this time he doesn't mind the challenge, the one-two-three-answer fast-left-flipper-right but now I'm sliding over to him again and a set of his muscles in his forearms clench and slow.

You mind if I take this one, I say, holding up a sock. It doesn't match anything else left behind. And what about these jeans? You don't need another pair of jeans, do you? Not with you never sitting down.

What? he says finally. I'm standing at his kicker elbow and the ball has dribbled into unreachable-land and I'm about to say my bit all over again when he makes a second What? But he still doesn't move his eyes from the scoreboard. After all, I've been curtseying in around corners for the better part of an hour, I'm due to go.

But I don't. I stand directly behind that kicker elbow, his power arm, and I say, Say, who's this? And then I shove a photo of a girl cut out of a magazine on top of his play.

The pinball man turns his head to me. Take that away, he says. Take that off my game. His voice is very even like he is frightened of that paper, like it is a spider.

No, no, no, have a look at it. Haven't you seen her before?

He picks up the slick, torn newsprint because seeing someone in newsprint is seeing someone famous, but instead he sees right away it's just a girl from a Sears catalogue in a red sweater.

Are you the father? I ask. You got her nose. The glasses woman is just one trailer on the other side of you.

The pinball man lets the newsprint fall back into my hands.

You get out of here, he says, and starts his free game.

It's not like it's really her but it looks like her, don't you think? I am talking to the machines by then, I am talking to the wall.

The score is in the nine digits by the time I get my bundle of leftover clothes all tied up and brush the soap off the washers and sort the slugs out of the drier change. I ask him again on my way out and I assume it is a Yes that he's said, out of shame or just to get me away, but no matter, I have this picture finally and I can tell by how he looked at it it is good.

I am on my way when Ernie comes up with one of his couch pillows, dirty in the seam plastic though maybe washable. Nice job on the fence, little lady, he says.

Good, I say. I tuck the clothes under the sweater I've got on.

The way I do it—kind of quiet—stops him. Where were you last night? he asks instead of asking about what's under the sweater. I was all stretched out last night, he says, star-watching from my sofa. I got the set just so on the inside, and I can hear the words if I jack it up. Whole lots of stars in swimsuits on the tube and where were you?

I went fishing, I say, pulling my sweater down more.

Fishing? There's no body of water anywhere around here except an alkali pool which of course is not for fish. Why do you say fishing?

He would press his hand to my forehead with that kind of voice if it were something he could cool down or dose up.

I guess I'm crazy, that's why. I shrug and back off, I turn toward my own place.

What you got there underneath? he asks, a little loud like I can't hear.

Socks, I say. With no mates. And lint, a lot of lint. It's from the washers.

Lint, he says, catching up. Let me see that. He puts down his cushion.

This is just useless stuff from the laundry, I say, opening my bundle.

He pushes the clothes this way and that. The old jeans have been stuck to the backside of the blower nearly since it was installed, he says, they are practically part of the room. You can have them though, he says.

I take my bundle back. See, I say, giving him the sight of my picture. There she is. I hold it up where he must see it.

He takes it. Look at that. Maybe she will be somebody when she fills out.

I scoop my clothes tight in one arm and take the picture back. That's okay, I say. You really think you haven't seen her before, running around here with the others?

A lot run around. Now if she were black or some other color, I might remember, but this here is not the case. I mean, these people move in every other week. You have only been here a short time. You don't know how many of the people are the same.

That's what's wrong, I say. But I bet a few stick.

Look, whatever your problem is isn't this place or however many people come and go, he says.

I say Yes with my head but that's all. Why doesn't anyone want to find her?

Ernie crumples up the picture as if he is getting rid of trash. Who can know what people want to find? People can cause you trouble for the things you find. Besides, don't you think I know what's going on around here?

No, I say. You are always at them with your aerial. What is her name, if you know so much.

Ernie picks up his pillow again. I've been to their baptisms when they got their names. I know more names than anybody here.

Yes, I say. What are they?

You just don't bother too many people about things, if you know what's good for you, he says, and he finds his way past me.

23

NIGHTS IN THAT DARK, the fence hung all over with leftover laundry, the jeans caught on one of the barbs as if leaping over and the owner skinnied out, the socks woven a little in and out of the plastic shreds, and all of it dripping with a rain that doesn't let up, a flood rain that had better not.

24

When the poker game ends with the letup of rain, not a soul shuffles chip grease further into the faded decks or picks at the chips that are left. The card players sit inside a screen house that is the kind that keeps bad bugs out but not the cold, they sit inside in their parkas and mittens and play on a sawhorse-and-door table and just stop when the rain stops.

Nobody bothers to turn to watch out the screen at the last of the rain. They stretch and rub their gloved and mittened fingers together and finish beers.

Beyond the card game, in the grey light that smokes up at the utter end of day when children refuse to come home or dry off or even look up for fear of night, real night, one person is shaken by another by the shoulder and the shake that is made travels all the way to the woman's head, which bounces hard and makes her barely able to talk. Not that she says much.

I'm almost sneezing and holding it. It's not so good to sit inside too long with all my wet nests so I stand out where soon spots of dry will show.

He's saying, I told you I was coming.

More than once he says this.

Where are the flowers? she asks, out of her chin and rattling teeth. Where's the hello kiss?

He laughs. I've got what you need, he says. He holds up a bag as if it's flowers.

Just not the kids, she says and starts to straighten up.

Oh, he says, letting her shoulder go so quick she staggers, now you're fussy about the kids?

To hell with you, she says with an unsure voice, not even with her voice, mostly with her hand. With you, she says.

I'll take care of them instead of you, he says. He leans close to her. I will take them, I will play dad, I will get the court to give them to me.

She pulls away hard and walks off, fast and angry.

I'll give you five minutes, he says to her back, turning himself like he's going to count it out, as if it were a game. You decide.

She passes my trailer, she stomps through the mud that is fresh everywhere, that globs up her legs she is stomping so hard and fast. But when she gets to her own trailer, she doesn't go in, she rests her head on its flank.

He walks closer but not especially to her. She hears him and swings herself around and is going to say what to him when she slips in all that mud and in trying to save herself, rams the card players' tent with her hand.

A stake flies out and the sawhorse table with a whipped-cream-and-jello treat now balanced on it topples with the two diners beside it still chatting cards and rain. What the hell?

She uprights herself fast even though it is mud, so fast it's as if she actually feels his five minutes ending, and she says, Sorry! at the still thrashing whipped-creamed card players, then she heads off, shouting with what seems the same breath, Kate! get your ass over here.

He comes along, smiling with his not-old face.

Now the cards have spilled too. Someone carrying a rag to blot the cream hits the just-righted table in a swerve to miss someone's fork and most of the deck falls to the floor. While Help! Help! is still what they're saying, some old woman takes the gum from her mouth and sticks it on a stick to pick up those cards.

25

I'M AT THE FENCE, SMELLING smoke, and pulling off plastic. The cows stand ten feet away, doing their cow flops, their thistle-mouthings, their sideways weed sniffs at what weeds are left. They are arranged in cow rectangles of matching red and white, no one cow fully out of the arrangement but none of them lined up so you can see all the way around them at once. It is from behind one of these rectangles that the smoke rises.

Sometimes fires are set to help things, to get growth going. This is more likely a fire from a dump that is not too far off, a fire to get rid of things. I watch the cows eat under the faint brown and grey cloud and they eat quietly and steadily and unannoyed. They must not mind fire or smoke.

I pull paper off the fence, something with crosswords all written out on it.

There's a cough.

A cough could have drifted in over the cows' shufflings. I stare hard at the herd. The herd hasn't heard, or minded. One of them stares back at me, a cow's stare, one that wonders at instead of sees, and it twitches off flies at the same time.

The smoke smokes.

I drop my bag of picked trash. I climb over the fence, a climb without grace and nearly without skirt, my slip hem catching because I try to be fast. Come here, I say. Come.

Like a dog's come.

The cows don't move.

My dress whips my legs, my hair flies in front of me while I dodge the cow rectangles and try looking at their undersides. Where else could a girl be?

I find burnt circles. Where kids have dropped matches? The wet grass has stopped the burning so there's no more flame, just black circles. Give me those matches, I say into the cows, but there's no one hugging the tits I can find, or behind legs, or behind me. I turn fast to check. The cows shuffle and take time to part. It's dangerous to play with matches, I say, not too loud. I say it again, louder, and the cows start. Then I shout, Be careful! and swallow all the dust the cows make, leaving.

The walk back is brief because I'm already saving her in my head, I've already marched up to the fence and pressed my way through the barb again and then turned to the mother's trailer and knocked.

But I haven't. There in the front is the kids' matching toy cup, in a hard plastic color that never goes grey in the sun, the handle in a shape that reminds me of my smile, that too cheerful smile.

I do not knock. The door is open and Kate and Collin and the baby sit in front of a television, the shades half down which shows off the new line of electricity filling their TV with blue for their faces, and other colors. I ask them, Where is your mother?

After some time I wonder if I have put sound behind my voice or if the television has sucked my voice into its own. Where is your mother? I ask again, and the children don't so much as move their eyes in my direction.

Fear? Or television power? I bang on the trailer's insides, where metal shows through, on cupboard doors and broom closets without doors, on tables strewn with dirty silver and half-eaten over-frosted cupcakes.

The mother enters from the bedroom, the only room with a door except the bathroom. She's in a robe. Get out of here, she says.

The bedroom door doesn't slam shut behind her, it

bounces the way trailer doors do and shows McGuire in a lounge position behind her and more flesh than a cop should show someplace outside his house. But he waves as if this is the way he is supposed to be and even gets dismissal into that wave.

Get out, says the mother again. Trash lady.

She's got matches out there. She sets fire, I say.

The mother kicks the bedroom door's outside shut better this time, and it locks with a ding.

Go on, get out and I mean get, says the mother.

I don't leave. I stand in my dirt-edged sundress, my hands in unraveling mittens newsprint black and with lots of slip showing.

See out there? I say. See the smoke?

The mother faces the window and can't help but look. That's nothing, she says. Just all those stupid cows and some smoke.

That's not true, I say. It's dangerous.

The mother fumbles in the pocket of her bathrobe and finds her own matches, finds cigarettes. Who cares what you think?

Kate, I say. She cares.

The mother lights up. Really? she says.

Isn't that right, Kate? You want your sister back, don't you, Kate?

Kate keeps watching, her face pulsing with TV light. The other children look and look away and look back. What sister? Kate says finally.

See? says the mother. Now get out.

Before she can step toward me, McGuire falls out of the bedroom on his arm, his belt buckle almost done, his shirttail dragging its flap, the bedroom door nearly ripped off its hinges because he tried to dress himself in that small space left without putting the bed up.

Whoo-ee, he says, righting himself. Trash lady, you do stink.

He tucks himself in, fingers back his hair.

I beg your pardon, I say. I see Kate let one tear escape down her face without turning, without blinking at the screen.

Go on, get out of here, says McGuire, putting his hand on the mother as if in protection or anger. But the mother turns away from the window, away from the man and the television and the kids, to the wall where's there's nothing, not even a calendar.

If she don't want us, says the mother, I got no way to hold her.

I know if I ask now, I will hear it all. She wants to tell, with her eyes on the wall. But it is not the child she is upset about, that I know. She is the one who is not grown up, who needs things a child can't even know to get for her, the child who gets kicked because she doesn't know, the child who gets nothing over and over because who has anything? And what else? No, I can't ask because then I will hear what will tear a child from her mother so well and surely, and that will fire me up, that will make me remember and burn.

26

WHO KNOWS WHAT THE SKY could do? says Ernie. There it is, sure, but why doesn't it tip over and spill out its waxy white hot stars onto us just because we're looking at them, just because we're out here, sitting on my goddamn great couch?

With a stop in the rain and out on his couch, Ernie has just now noticed the real stars and has dragged out his heater to keep us warm. I say, Remember when that family allowed us a night light?

Ernie rubs his head in his hands as if it helps him remember. Okay. The night light was just a way they cared about us falling over all their stuff.

I shift in my fold-up chair pulled up right next to his

couch, I shift closer and kiss him. The night is quiet all around us, except for the heater trying to heat.

He won't come to my place now. The plastic that bells off the front fills with fall wind and lets it go. An iron lung is what he thinks of it, the head of a girl and a big machine making her breathe, and if he comes in, he says, he will have to give up breathing too.

The trick for that family we were with, I say after a while, is what color eyes. They had to be black. You didn't have black eyes. That's what they had, what they wanted. Black eyes.

I could have had that color. I could have been anyone because I was no one, he says. No pictures, nothing. He runs his fingers through the few books he's always selling from his pockets. He pours himself half a cup from the coffee in the mayo jar he has sitting on the sill and drinks it before the rest of the jar coffee has stopped its sloshing.

The cricket in the laundry plays its legs.

I don't say, You were a someone, you had a trailer court. You even had a grandfather. Instead I say, Remember how that parent looked the day we put her shoe in the soup?

I don't remember, he says.

I almost slide off my chair, the parent with her shoe in the soup in my head, and how she tried to laugh it off—was that ever funny.

My laughing stops. You pounded a stake in the ground with a hammer. You said you could always come back to it—that was on the day you left. The stake had been for tomatoes and had a place where both our names were written on it in red pen. You put it up in the back, against the chainlink where I could see it from the room I was in. But what was this stake? A piece of wood in one place. The parent ran over it with the lawnmower a week after you left and I got blamed.

A stake, he says. What do you know. He's pulling apart a carcoat cord or one from bathing trunks, something that he's found tangled in his pocket with the chance books.

It makes me nervous for you to do that, I say. Quit it, I say, and look around. I think you'll get to the end of that cord and then what, I say.

He wrinkles the top half of his face. The bottom half frowns. I remember angels, he says. He liked angels.

He? The parent at the home?

Yes, says Ernie, very quiet. I remember a lot of white sheets pushed over and around. I once hid under the striped sheets but it was no good. I forgot the pillow case, its white.

He did it to you too? I pinch my mouth together.

Ernie nods in the dark. My angel, he said.

Why, that clinches it, I say. The worst ever.

The cord is all undone.

I say, Want some food? I have a can I could open.

You are such a cook, I can't say yes, he says, and now he laughs. I'll just take a leak, if you don't mind. You go on and eat what you need to.

He crosses the mud of the court in the chill dark.

I find the can I want inside and go out and put it on my table.

It was a mistake that we ever stayed together in that home. Sometimes not even brothers and sisters of the same family of a certain age were allowed to stay together, let alone children not brother and sister. But our papers were lost, mine somewhere and his somewhere else, so we did stay together because the people who lost them didn't want either of us themselves and the closest place to put us permanently was having a secret outbreak of typhoid and the next closest needed money to get into. There was only one place.

It was in that home that I unrolled toilet paper in a straight line from his mattress in the basement all the way up to where I slept with the spare china hutch and the extra fans on a bed that they said would soon be repaired. I unrolled it just to show them we could play brother and sister, that we really did know how to be together. They wouldn't let us be together during the day so I thought I could make them understand by being with him at night like a sister, telling him stories, reading to him.

I spent the whole night reading to him, me, a ten-year-old

so skinny my breathing out words into sentences puffed me up like some lizard. He could not read the way I could. He lay on my lap to listen, in pajamas without a shirt because that is what some home before said to do, that only cowards afraid of gunshot wounds or arrows cover their hearts at night. Or it could have been a habit from his own father but he didn't think so, his father didn't want him and who tells stories like that to kids they don't want?

As soon as I closed the book, he started to tell me his stories and not just the one about the cat. They started out small, I remember, out of a marble dropped from a boy's bag, and ended in an unbeknownst land full of dead giants. There was one where we were caught inside this marble, rolling along into a good, sunny place, and when it broke against a tree, a real boy and a real girl came out of it, no more made of wood or rubber or that stuff they make pans out of, but two real people.

Of course we were beaten silly the next day, but neither of us would say who unrolled all that paper. After all, it led equally to him and to me—the rest of the roll I put back on the roller in the bathroom. He was so happy, like me, to have someone who was moving from home to home and knew how it felt to be a form first, then a boy or girl, that he didn't tell.

Now I know I unrolled the paper to get out of envy, to

release myself from that certain pain I had after he told me about the court and its promise, even though what I wanted just as much was a brother to read to.

And, of course, after a certain number of beatings and deprivings, he was sent away because of course a girl couldn't cause the kind of harm that the toilet paper was pointing to. I was sent away too but not first. Not until the man who was the father wanted me.

As an angel.

I let the catfood burn a little so it will taste like something. The cats know enough now not to insist until the pan is empty of my bits, and then they fight at my feet for what they can still lick.

He has been gone a long time for a pee when I see his flashlight. His face is not in the light, then it is, as he pumps his arms, coming closer.

He looks like a spook and then not. I laugh.

I didn't think you were a crazy person, he says when he hears me, I thought you were all right like before. Even when I didn't recognize you, I thought you were all right and not crazy. He puts the light on me as if I am someone he has never noticed.

I am not crazy, I say, although I have never said that to anyone before. I just have my own mind. Now, I do not need all this light. Turn your light off.

He keeps waving it around me. What about all the wet

stuff I just saw on the fence? What's all that about? A joke? Or are you making fun of me?

I am not. I don't say more.

He starts pacing in front of my card table, now and then swinging the light into the dark. I might as well tell you, he says, your neighbor's been on me day and night about the food you've been putting under your trailer. Now, what are you putting food under your trailer for, anyway? He stops, the *o* of his light like it could cut the trailer where there are no bags holding it together, where it is still whole, and he bends down and shines his light underneath.

I mind my own business, I say. So should she.

Maybe I'm just dreaming, I say to myself, he says, standing up and shaking his light as if it's not lighting what it should. Maybe I'm just pissing and dreaming. Or maybe somebody is playing a trick on her, I think. Or there is some big wind I don't know about that comes along. Don't go and dress her down because she's got a lot to do around here with all of this, I say to myself.

He turns off his light. His face goes dark and silent. It's like a door opening to a basement I can smell. I put my feet up on the cinderblock to eat my food.

But he won't let me.

Put that down, he says. You and me are going to have a look together, we are going to figure this out.

He has me by the arm, he has the flashlight pointing the

way. Why should you stay, he says, pulling me along, if you make fun of me?

I could say, Friend, I could say, Why not?

The flashlight picks out his wet pee spot but doesn't stay still—the fence isn't full, the light searches for the full part, both ways.

The fence is bare.

I don't stay to hear his surprise, however, not even to hear a sorry or two, or him scratch his head, the light in his hand scratching the all-around dark over him. I grab that light away and force myself through the fence and run into the full dark.

Hey, shouts Ernie, and he runs after me, tripping on the plant tufts, or the sand-slick, or mud, and cursing.

I run into the gully, my feet splayed and tripping down the grade to where the cows might be but are not, then over again to where surely they stand but don't, then I stop.

He gains on me halfway, then he stops where I do and takes the light from my hand.

Careful, he says. The cows have been all over, watch your feet. Now what? he says, shining the light back on me. The stuff on the fence was there, wasn't it?

You saw the fence, I say. What do you think? But I don't look at him, I look away and there's wet on my cheek in the light spill.

I could save her, I say. Point that light over there and maybe you'll see her.

He moves the light off my pinched-up eyes down to my front where my hands don't know what to do.

Give me a break, I say. I can't stop the tears.

Okay, okay. The fence is all clean so everything is okay. Okay?

Come on, he says. He lets the light fall as he gathers me. Cut the crying. Even when you were with me and young, you didn't cry.

How do you know what I did? I stumble along. I learned to cry right after you went, I say, and it was a good thing to do, I say.

I manage to steer the light in his hand by bumping him with my body on the way back. I can't surprise him again and grab it. But this way whatever I see, he sees too. There's the herd, I don't have to say when we're there in a gully fold with just cows' eyes looking back, lamps that reflect, Don't trip.

You go to bed, says Ernie after he holds the barbs for me. That's what I'm going to do. Seeing those clothes all hung up, well, he says, I'd like to believe I never did see them. Maybe all I need bad is sleep.

Tell me the story about the marble, I say just as his flashlight shows where he is going alone. That one, I beg, all my tears held and swallowed.

Story? he asks. You mean like a lie, that kind of story?

Like in the home, I say. Like on one of those nights on that couch. I'm facing the gully since I know the dark there will comfort me. I wipe my face with my hand, which I then run over a torn piece of sundress.

I don't know stories, he says. You got the wrong one for stories.

What he says goes away with his light.

27

FIRST THE CRYING, THEN the baby's head, then Kate's under the baby's head. I see from my place as a rock that the baby is not holding on to her back as well as he might and he's slipping as Kate rears up onto a flat part. Hold him a second, she says.

Freddie puts down the club he is smoothing with a kitchen knife and takes the baby off her back, but not without looking around first, in case there are boys who would laugh, for example, Collin. In thanks, the baby tries to bite him, but Freddie's fast, he knows about this baby and puts the club's smoothest part in the way of the baby's mouth.

Thanks. I can't do this at home. Kate pulls out a slip of aloe from her pocket that must be stolen it is so bunched up and broken, and peels it to the wet and lays the leaf leather against the baby's cheek where it's swollen and the eye bloodshot. The baby cries when she touches him with the leaf and tries hitting her and hits Freddie instead, who looks at the baby and his big tears that make the leaf hard to stick on.

You will get better, Kate tells the baby. Look at me.

The baby stops crying and looks and cries more, cries because she's not telling the truth, cries because he's been smacked so hard for crying, cries because crying makes him cry.

I want to take that baby and put him back together. I could do that but so could Kate. I sit with my knees to my chin, silent as rock, here to watch the few court lights come on.

The crying goes on and off. They take turns holding him until it's dark. Once she asks if there was a count on the bus coming home and he says no, but Mrs. Warner put a tick by her name in the book. Once he asks her if he gave her a ride home after. At least, he says. For an answer, she takes out a bag of candy, the pellet kind in different colors, and neither of them touches it after she lays it on a rock, not even when the baby wants it, hitting his head on Freddie's shoulder, not even when they know he would suck it and smile.

It's dark enough, Kate says when the crying becomes all there is around them. He helps to haul the baby the distance back, the baby whose legs, stretched out, reach down his back to his knee creases. I come too because it's time. I'm wheezing and noisy and they turn to see if I make it, as if I am a pet that follows. When they reach the court, the baby's asleep.

Collin is sitting outside their trailer in the damp cold dark, holding a popsicle close to the color of the baby's bruises. He doesn't call Freddie anything, not even Whimphead, though Freddie still carries the baby. What Collin does say to him is, I like it, about the club that is laced to the loop on Freddie's belt.

Freddie sinks beside him to talk about how he will break the biggest bottle, even root beer-size. Kate pries the baby off his back, then trudges with him in her arms to the steps where her mother is calling, Food! Dinner! as if it is her only demand.

28

ALL THE FAT FLIES DOING last minute mating on the water surface of the windmill tank have sunk into its chill green slime or hang their fatness under the tank lip, quivering with the little life they have left, waiting for cows to come for a last drink of the day, to bite them.

And so the night starts its long haul. Eventually people come and go with their outside car lights and then their inside ones, but the dark is the end of them. Then, at the ass end of the night, when even the flies in the gully tank stop mating and bugs and worms have chased each other to death, one of the people, a man, retches out a trailer window behind which children scream and scream, and then he leaves that same trailer in a hulking.

He drops or tosses something close to me on my outside

chair where I sit when I can't sleep. He retches again and then straightens up and returns to the trailer, throws his fists against it in punches that sound like someone wanting to know if the door is hollow or not, not like the door is in the way. Sweetheart, he whines, then he walks down the steps beside the trailer's picture window, with a curtain that someone lifts as he passes, then he growls out curses and warnings like three wishes no one wants to know and a We'll just see about that.

I slide that dropped thing over, and put it with its match into my pocket, both of them now useless and melted. Then there's the tock of the laundry cricket to the shuffle of the man's footfalls, his side-shamble against the dark things in the court because the Xmas lights are off and there are no stars tonight, none to interest Ernie who earlier watched on his couch in case they came out and fell, the couch that the man walks into where it extends past the rig. His Oof! wakes the pinball man who's camped there, all stretched out on his way to his own place that he will eventually get to because he knows how Ernie will scream at the sight of his sneakers smack on top of his vinyl covered pillows, and better to have him wonder about the sneaker dirt and blame others. But when the man makes his Oof! the pinball man just turns over and so does Ernie, inside, turning away from a night noise that doesn't quite startle.

So the man goes on, more angry than before, cursing and

cursing, and when finally he takes out his keys, they drop against his car door, so he's cursing again, this time on his hands and knees, cursing and grabbing for them somewhere in that underneath dark.

Cold and dirty, he finds them lying next to his groveling chin. As he straightens up, fingering his handful, he looks around a little, looks around as if he hears or sees something in the black late night. A child does start to cry again but that's nothing, that's not noise. He himself jingles louder, reaching with his wet keys for his car handle, fitting one into the lock and turning it.

What's next is a razor light that runs through him so quick he jerks and falls before the keys do, a light so hot there's instant smoke from his nylon jacket and a stink. He does twist and thrash and maybe what's next is a whack on the head for good measure. Or does the pole that is balanced so carefully with its cords dangling fall finally and hit him too hard?

The red light turning on top of the car is the same one that came with pencils for the children, the one that now turns its redness over the sprawled man who is no longer drunk, where those fat flies from the tank collect in joyful chorus with the sheriff, his deputy, and the people from the court. This spectacle is increased in wildness by McGuire having his hand always over his gun as if to protect the sheriff's notetaking, his thick black binder out and already a page full of incident.

It looks like a hit on the head to me and a burnt coat, says the sheriff. That's what I wrote down, but we'll have to wait for the coroner.

Ernie nods, two people over.

The power is wild around here, says McGuire. The company hasn't turned it on right.

Is that so? says the sheriff. Wasn't there someone who reported seeing a flash?

The crowd stares at each other instead of the body. I did, says the blind mechanic who looks at his feet, as if he could look. But it was the yelling, he says.

Someone is always yelling in the middle of the night, says Ernie.

I see, says the sheriff. No flash. Just the usual? the sheriff asks but really states, and takes a note. Where does all this usual yelling usually take place?

Oh, a long way off, says Ernie, glaring down the crowd at the mechanic. Could have even come from the highway, a middle-of-the-night kid's joyride.

The sheriff looks up from his labors on the note pad. Oh, he says, then why did this blind man here mention it?

Could you have McGuire relax a little? asks Ernie. After all, this is just an accident.

An accident? says the sheriff and writes that down. McGuire? Would you please cease and desist?

McGuire has been looking into the place where the bullets go, checking them and their nest. He has done this noisily because he doesn't really know how. It is his not knowing that makes the sound nerve-wracking, the tick and gravity of it. He quick shuts the gunback and shoves the tip into his holster.

According to what's been reported, the dead man frequented your trailer, Ma'am, says the sheriff. He was your husband?

The mother is right beside Ernie and Ernie has his hand on her arm tight as if she will bolt, but she is not sobbing or crying, she's keeping her eyes as wide as those girls in velvet paintings with the tears about to drop, and she tells the sheriff the man's full name and hers too and their dates of birth and of marriage. She tells him he sells locks on the road.

I see, says the sheriff, chewing at his pen tip. Yeah, he says. Did anybody else hear anything?

He was always arguing about this and that with her, says a neighbor, one of the card players.

We got that, says the sheriff.

He brought me things, says the mother. Flowers, she says.

Kate slips around to the front of her mother but what she offers is less protection than distraction: her face is covered with Band-Aids and she's shivering. Her mother puts her hand on her head but doesn't look at her like the rest of us do.

For Chrissake, says the sheriff. What's wrong with the kid?

The mother widens her eyes because he is not noticing the tears she has coming down behind her big glasses, and then she looks at Kate and says, She cut herself.

All over her face? asks the sheriff.

All over, says the mother who pulls the hurt side of her daughter closer. One of the Band-Aids falls off with this pull and it shows a regular row of holes, the kind a barrette might make if it were heated, if people did these things, if people did them twice.

I stand across from her.

The sheriff hesitates and is looking at the mother when he says, Big guy, wasn't he? But he's talking to McGuire who is fooling in the mud near some footprints next to the body that is sticking out of the blanket someone has sacrificed.

Yeah, sir, big. When is that ambulance going to get here?

What's the hurry? asks the sheriff, closing his notebook. They waited long enough to call us.

McGuire laughs and lifts one muddy foot, then another.

The ambulance lets loose a scream not so far away along the highway.

Sheriff, I say, and I have kept my big mouth shut all this time, Sheriff, can I talk to you?

The sheriff and everyone else crane around to see me.

She's the one who thought there was an extra kid here the last time, says McGuire to the sheriff. She's the trash lady.

I remember. The sheriff sighs and the leather on him creaks as he turns toward me. Ma'am, he says, If you've got an idea about who did it, just come on down to city hall and we'd love to hear all about it but right now I can't take a statement, I have this ambulance to contend with.

The sheriff waves at the ambulance as it backs around his car, waving with relief that it misses all but a little sideswipe, and because this body will be taken away and dealt with by someone else. Instead of moving for the ambulance, the crowd tightens around the body, no one wanting to miss a single glimpse of it exposed, except for the mother who backs away because she can't watch and must watch so much.

Kate wriggles out of her mother's grip to stay at the front where she can see him rolled over. Maybe she needs to make sure he's not just sleeping the way he would sleep, and when she is sure about that—the way the arm is so stiff it looks like it never was bent and for sure like it will never be now—she punches Freddie hard in his shoulder where he stands beside her and then she runs away.

I watch two men take the motor from the car and the lock samples for evidence. At least that's what they say they're doing. I say nothing else to anyone but I look at the earth the body lay on top of and see how there is not a trace of him at all, only mud that looks like any other.

29

FREDDIE IS SMASHING bottle after bottle of the bottle garden Kate was digging to look like mine, smashing each one of the bottle bottoms with his fancy club. He lifts and drops his club onto the buried bottom dark green where it is full of earth light and it is soon all just glass. A cut spot blooms on his arm.

I stop him.

I catch the club as it swings back, and I hold it. He turns to hit me with it sideways, to hit at anything. I let go and he hits the soft ground around me a few times, then drops to the ground himself.

Behind him is the mother's trailer. There is nothing to say about the mother's trailer except that the door is open and its insides are empty and no one is there and there's nothing in it. I go from room to room, all three of them, looking. Crumbs, hair, and dust show what there was from before, a toaster, a curling iron, a phone book.

Freddie is still in the yard when I come out. Where? I ask. Where did they go?

After I shake him to stop what must be sobbing, he says. She took them in the night and just left.

The couple of play cups aren't anywhere around. Not even that. I turn to the gully with its herd moving as lazy as ever. Freddie smacks another bottle.

Get out of there!

That's Ernie, furious at Freddie and his glass breaking. Freddie doesn't bother to move, seeing him, instead he's hanging over the broken glass as if he's watching how the sun has begun to pick on the pieces, as if it is everything he ever wanted to watch.

Go on, says Ernie, and then Freddie looks up at him and spits.

Ernie doesn't think of himself as a small boy with a lot of sadness the way he should but instead raises his arm to Freddie.

Freddie blinks up at him as if he is just a wall in the way.

Ernie beats him and beats him. I walk away from it since he can't hear me shrieking, he can't hear how the child doesn't cry but is hardening. He hears only himself, with the aerial at the end of his long arm cutting the air. Cry, goddammit, yells Ernie. Cry, cry.

But it's Ernie who's crying, Ernie who covers his face.

Freddie doesn't move when it's over, just Ernie, who walks off first, with the aerial broken. I am sitting behind my trailer in a crouch, watching, and so are others. We watch while Freddie sits up as soon as Ernie leaves, proud in his face that he has not moved, has not cried or run away. He is not a big boy but his standing up like that makes him tall. If he limps when he leaves it's because he wants to show how big what happened to him was, that it is no small thing he has suffered.

30

I PUT OUT FOOD. I MAKE a little tray from cardboard with pipe cleaners none too clean poked in so it suspends and that's where I put every dog and cracker I have, even seeds from the feeder that I smack open, seeing all the birds have gone south or home. I fasten it underneath and I wait.

It's a trap this time. I have a sheet I can throw out to stop her, a piece of rug she can sleep on. But all the time I hear frogs. They're loud and wrong, like the ones in the woodwork, like indigestion. They call from sand emptied from shoes, out of an upturned dishpan, in a chorus so big who cares if they're done mating—they're warning.

It hits like a spatula splat.

Wind presses the water down, wind puts in currents as it

falls, there could be a sea in that wind, falling. I peer through my plugged-up window, and hear extra rain tap outside where my table sits, each drop filling in the space between its four legs. Underneath the trailer where the tray hangs is filling in fast. I go out and hook the cleaners a little higher on the tray, but it doesn't stay dry long, not with a frog warning like that.

Ernie bangs on my door and says there's a bit of a break in the S of the land between here and the town, it's more like a C. Just don't come out until we say so or you hear a whistle, he says.

You stay, he says.

Loose trash that ought to be on the fence starts to wash by, then the feeder that I cracked open, then part of a tool shed old ladies favor turned on its side. I don't think too much about all this—trash is trash in wind or water—until I see Ernie's couch adrift, its plaid vinyl trailing a rope that surely Ernie fixed to the tire of his place.

My trailer is too close to the gully. If I don't give it some weight, I will soon follow. I haul the top cinderblock step out of the wet and heave it into the center inside.

In the institution once, the TV showed a tornado passing a few feet from the wall where the picture people told me about was hung. People told me the tree in that picture was the same as the tree out the window. The TV kept us watching during its whole uprooting, we were that full of fear with that kind of storm. All that TV fear made people stand at the window and lean toward the picture, made someone play the piano that stood under the window, unplayed for all the time I stayed there until then, played then standing up, looking, while the tree lifted itself outside, the only place that the picture and what was out the window was the same. The tree went right out of the window and from then on, some of the people drifted, nothing angled or dangerous, but for days. The picture was out for them.

I am glad the window I have with all its bags does not match anything, inside or out.

The rain is too hard to hear Ernie's whistle, this pounding of rain the opposite of whistle.

Cows float by and they're not swimming, noses held high. I think they are just dogs and then some new part parts the water, a rump, a tail afloat. They float not in their herd, they come one or two, they've come apart.

The rain falls in sheets so nothing is now visible. If it were a bad TV, it would be snow.

Then I hear a whistle and I put my foot out, forget there is one block less and fall into the river. But it's not so bad, I can float. I float with a vomit of components and broken bits of plastic foam and a very special magazine with all the latest dos, I float to people by the fence. For once they are standing by the fence, standing because the water there is not so high.

I fight to my feet. I stand beside them and I see why else they stand.

She is tangled in like all the rest. People are pulling the plastic from around her, people are cutting the sweater loose. She has her mouth shut to keep out what is coming, what is pushing her. Or is she about to call out but she's having trouble with the fence?

A cat has been on her already. Pieces of her are gone, important pieces, and she has no face to speak of except for the mouth that is so shut.

Tell the cat our real true names and it will eat everything.

I didn't say my name.

I see how the cat could be caught on the fence with her, so afraid, and I see how it could fight the fence, and since she's there too, it fights her too, and since it's hungry—it's always hungry—it eats her.

Our real true names.

I press her to me, barb and all.

People quiet even more. They let me weep.

I have to be helped away. Ernie keeps ahold of a bottlebrush he has found as he helps me and its whiskers press into my arm, that's how hard he helps.

31

THE TRUCK DRIVES RIGHT UP and two men with muscles you see even under their sweatshirts swing down from the cab and ask if I am who I am and let's see I.D. I say, Yes I am but that the flood we had took away every scrap of what you might call I.D.

The truck is sinking in the last mud of the driveway, its hubs are going down, and while one of the men kicks at those hubs, the other says, Anyway, we need you to sign.

And they have seen the slip showing, the sundress sliding even under the two sweaters, and still they want me to sign? I stare at them in wonder. Where is that paper? they ask each other. They both end up back in the cab, opening up compartments, looking under seat mats. We get so tickled, one of them says, when we make a delivery like this, we get all excited.

I sign the paper they find though I take my time about it and do it quietly and don't ask why. It's nothing bad, they say. On the contrary, they say, and laugh as if contrary is such a funny word. They go open up the back. She didn't need to be present, one says to the other, dragging out the pallet.

The Frigidaire stands on its own in the back. It could be a room with a door you could enter, it is so big. Someone has to win, the other one says. I see him eye my place which has more plastic in its holes than ever before. How will they get it to fit?

Ernie must have been ironing because the shirt he's tucking in sends steam out from under his down vest. What is the number? he asks. Don't you need a number? he says to the men who are grunting and pushing.

No number necessary, they say, checking their records. Just the delivery, they say and they nod. They shoulder the monster, a frost-free even, and dolly it all the way inside to where there could be a kitchen. There they open its door, put water in a box, plug it in where I have rigged up my own juice, and then, the way people do with an appliance, pat it on the handle.

The hum is so lovely.

I go over to it and press up to its side. Ice crashes already.

You have some luck, says Ernie who can just squeeze himself in.

No one remembers any other.

Sundress

It's a terrible thing to be kicked out. I hold the kicked-out birdcage, the kicked-out double geranium, and the kicked-out dog. But after we look at all this kicked-out stuff, there really isn't much we want. I mean those pillows have seen heads. So we leave the birdcage and flower with the ironing boards in the hope of Stayprest and recycling, and go for a walk, Ernie in his most impressive Just-A-Moment-Sir suit, which he put on as a sort of armor this morning, and I in my sundress, off-the-shoulder, with a pattern swirly and close, one that if you look too long at, well, instead of thanked, you get kicked out.

The walk goes into the subway and out to the suburbs. Ernie walks with the dog's leash held high and his saggy chin tilted, scenting promise because what else? I bring up the rear with the two mostly empty bags bumping syncopated on a carrier up and down the high curbs they have here. We don't go far. Ernie comes up with a couple of nearly-last bills and buys sodas, something with a lot of escape, he says, and we sip them outside the store, looking at wide lawns and white houses.

We don't talk. I know Ernie from the beginning, from when we crossed once in foster homes. We had luck and not luck after leaving fifty years between us and them, and now I can see, even with dime-store bifocals, Ernie is already thinking up some new way, taking in the neighborhood with his careful old-man looks over soda.

After a while he calls a taxi. I am not surprised at the why, not to mention the where, for those are the very, very last bills he is now waving. This Ernie is quick as well as silent. I am seated inside before I hear him say, Three times around the block and make it snappy.

We stop in front of the house we'd stared at over sodas and pull right into the driveway. Ernie pops out and surveys the short walk to the door, all mystery and smiles. The driver says as I whip out the two suitcases, They're not home, and slips his gears into reverse.

We are, says Ernie and pays him.

The driver looks at me in my sundress, then he takes his

time backing out but finally does gun off when Ernie settles the bags on the front step. Then Ernie pats me on my bare shoulder and says, I'll be just a minute, and ducks out to the stucco-front neighbors.

But what exactly does he say to the blonde with curls down to here and a face of collapsed Saran Wrap to have her hand over the house keys? To me not more than a minute later he says, We're the Olsen's first cousins, and tosses his almost white, anybody-cousin hair out of his part to open the door with the key.

While he gets the bags, I like it. I like the dark wood, the books, the lot of things to dust. There is a place for the rag under the sink and secret spots for the laundry. When I open the fridge, it is so empty it's like a bulldozed half building, but the pantry is walk-in, olives and sherry. Not like the last with its locks, with its May-I-this-and-that, its curtsey and shuffle.

Being help is the foster home forever.

Hey, Ernie, I yell, handling a quart of homemade piccalilli. But Ernie is out.

From the picture window I catch him, changed into his only other outfit, patched dungarees, wringing a wrench against the neighbor's stuck X. The woman of the stucco waves at me as soon as Ernie fixes it, wiping his hands and wrench on his clean shirt front, then accepting her invite to come in, wash up, and no doubt eat cookies. The woman at the window has cookie in her Saran Wrap face, not sex, which is flatter.

He goes in.

I don't panic at being so elsewhere so fast. I know Ernie. Ernie will talk us up. We will stay the night. The night is something. I open cocktail wieners and feed them singly to the dog who likes the smell of dark wood and low books but does not mark anything, not once. When Ernie comes back, we agree, night is something.

But we are there weeks and weeks. I take out videos on Saturdays from the pack of coupons I find by the console and make popcorn for the neighborhood kids, who don't even put their feet on the sofa. Right by the video is the Olsen's address in France which I keep clean, in a sort of shrine, away from the butts. I also take good care of the lawn, and I ask, Did Olsen really mean water three times a week? as if it is on a list. To the boy who does have a list, I feed Oreos and we never see again, except once, riding his bike and waving while Ernie's getting at the cracks in the driveway and scrubbing the oil spots. For everyone else Ernie fixes dishwashers, radiators, computers, any of those -er things. And takes nothing for it. I have words with him as usual, but he says, Give and it will come back. It is true, we get invitations nearly daily in lieu, and two old fridges which we sell as if unused. And when we visit, Ernie smokes out the boy-part in each husband where the talk locks on small parts or their dads' cars.

The ladies love the dog. All grin and no bite, it lures them off a lawn they are dressing or even tuning a headset, makes them bend at the knees and pet it. All I have to do is stand by that dog and they forgive my sundress with that pattern and its troubles.

It is on a Friday, a big day for waving and helping, for parading the dog and going to dinner, with the sun outside so hot in the late afternoon the neighbors have their blinds down and so don't see how we stop puttering and dusting when the phone rings.

Now we don't answer the phone ever. We tell people they have the machine on and we don't want to lose messages so it is just us, listening. But this is the ring we'd been expecting, a Mina something saying how she looks forward to seeing Mr. Olsen on Monday.

I haven't mentioned how little the neighbors look forward to seeing their neighbors. I try always to stay positive, people can feel it. But the Olsens are so unlike us, they say, you two are really so nice and how did they, they wonder, get so different. They even suggest we rent a bungalow just blocks off that would do so well, they say, for a couple active like us so we don't have to go back to Florida where we live in one of those wretched old people condos. Condos, I snort. But I let Ernie talk, just as I memorize the albums of pictures on the dresser and can speak on them. It is clear it is us the neighbors want, not them, the ones who are coming.

We drop off handwritten notes at all the doors Ernie has fixed and more, the ones who have asked for him but can't yet be fit in, and we put out potato chips and tonic I find in the basement closet. Then we paint up a sheet with *Surprise!* across it, a twin of one I'm making another sundress from.

All the kids come and watch what they want on video and all the adults clutch their last-minute repairs, small items like clocks and candy thermometers. And the man with the now-blinking electric eye brings the liquor that goes with the tonic.

Then the driveway is parked full, and the car that stops across the street and the bewildered couple who slam it shut are the right ones to greet the silence of the hidden crowd with the banners unfurling *Welcome Home, Cousin!* and of course our *Surprise!* but we don't see it, me in my gloves from wiping down doorknobs and Ernie with the suitcases still quite light settled on the street, leaning way out for the taxi we have called and is sure to come.

Just the dog doesn't want to.

I Dreamt He Fell Three Floors and Lived

THE REST OF THE WORLD pretends it is normal. A few birds cough up from the black-budded trees, two cars miss each other. Looking out the window, away from the bed, I begin to swell, filling the whole room. The nurse has a hard time getting to my son, and my mother is almost squeezed out of the room entirely. It's that I'm allergic to death, I think it's a reaction. Then, pop, I need a Hershey's and a bathroom, but that's it. Dad says I have to live with it.

Okay.

I look around at all these people stuffed in the tiny green room. Hospitals are for the modern, small family or for getting them smaller, not the bumper crop we have. They sit in chairs stolen from Detox and look at me. Who's taking care of the dog? I think to say.

Angie, says my second sister. Tacos twice a day.

With hot sauce. Honest. That is the dog-feeder herself, my third sister, holding a *Post* on her lap that has slipped. It shows me, my blonde hair framing a Munch moment, my hands clamped to the side of my face.

Laughter pitches from me, a whole lot of green leaves falling for no reason, what must have happened outside. I sit up in my chair. What is this, day three?

My next-to-last brother, leaning up against the wall, stretches, but has the sense not to say. The Yes comes from Mom, the Yes she uses after someone exclaims, So many children! As the eldest, I am the one who counts them. I learned to count first. I am not good at counting backwards. Blast off, I want to say now. Instead I ask, Is it okay to take off my clothes and rub my face in the dirt and howl?

It's winter, says my brother.

That's how much they take me seriously.

Okay.

The machine overhead practices its single red line. The nurse tells me I have another ten minutes to decide, then takes all my son's thin chart with her.

Didn't you go to Prague last summer? I ask the third sister.

Year before.

He made a turret out of blocks the other day, I say. He hurt his finger when they all came down. No keystone. I touch his cool, perfect finger, then pretend to have a headache.

Where is that doctor? That is my mother again.

Thick ropes of green, the wall paint, straighten out in front of me. I say, What I'd like is another Hershey's.

Someone looks relieved and volunteers to fetch one.

There is that much more air in the room when he leaves. With more air, I can turn my head, I can see my husband in a schlump in the chair beside me. He makes a tiny smile the size of an apostrophe, but he isn't the father. The father won't come to the hospital. He is too upset. Instead, he gives the papers the school photo which hardly resembles what lies before us now.

My own dad is standing behind my husband's chair, using it as a sort of barricade, to keep what is happening on the bed at bay. He doesn't cry, however, unlike everybody else here, even the nurses. Instead, getting out of the taxi this morning, he falls on a tree guard and loses two teeth. He can't even smile.

Let's sing, I say.

We know only two kinds of songs—carols and "I've Been Working on the Railroad." The carols all have to do with baby boys.

We're in full force, even Dad, moving his face around the stumps of his teeth, when the nurse comes back. I keep on singing while she hands me forms that read Corneas,

Kidneys—all the spares. These aren't my favorites anyway, I say, then get the hiccups.

The next day we wake, which is how I like to make a basically wordless party sound active. A little girl, not one of my son's friends, arrives last, clutching her father. She's so skittery I must be a lesson for her, a cautionary tale. The father smiles at her with a pride I'm not supposed to miss, which says, I have mine.

Look, I am the mother who did not take care of her child, I whisper. Boo! She runs away. To celebrate, I eat a whole plateful of kisses.

Someone says they ran the story in both papers. I saw them, I lie, looking away when he offers copies. Then I hear my mother tell that someone I'd recover. She says it the way you would if I had a cold with complications. I start to exude a toxic green chemical so everyone will stay away. It works. Only the sculptor hugs me. Then he tells the story of a kid who falls another hundred feet and survives.

Nobody my age has children. This is before the baby boom boomed. They just mill around, eating paté the way they do at openings. One of them blurts out that their dog died, is it like that? I start to swell again.

My husband likes parties. He is trying not to talk about anything, but I catch him discussing a movie. It had a good ending, he says, and can't go on.

The father is fighting with his girlfriend. I can tell because she is eating with her back to him, eating a lot the way I used to, to annoy him. He doesn't look to be too grief stricken, I notice. But then, he didn't have to sign for body parts. I'm the one with custody.

Without.

I myself have eaten only air and chocolate for the last few days. Not eating helps with the swelling. I get lighter easily and hit the ceiling fast, go as far away as I can without going. My family is going at six. Instead, they play Scrabble but keep the vocabulary limited, no past tense.

On some anniversary, I'm at the lawyer's and he says, What's wrong?

After I tell him, he reveals his wife was murdered ten years ago and he has their three kids.

So do I get mouse ears with the membership? I ask.

He looks at me as if I am a case on consignment. I won't charge you for telephone time, he says, and takes a call.

At night before I fall asleep—fall, I tell you, it's even a season—I see the distance between us and how I didn't catch him and I start to swell again, now as an ambulance, and all the sirens on the street join in riotous medley, with him whole inside me.

Doll

I DON'T TALK. I SLIDE DOWN as far under the covers as my nose still lets my breathing happen, so far down that I uncover my toes and can hardly hear anything, except for him. He talks and I see the picture from the church, the one of tongues in mid-air burning up, I see it through the covers. But the tongues are just the usual: mother's tongue, Bessie's tongue, his mean class of boys and girls who say anything, their tongues. Just not his tongue. His is going on while the nights gets going, his keeps the night from being as bad as all those tongues. Anyway, what he says isn't for me or about me.

Sure, I go to school, I hear Mom and Bessie and silence when all my trying at school goes wrong, even though people think potholders are easy for girls, like spelling. He thinks this too, talks about how they are coming at him with hooks, the girls, and how the right letters come up out of their mouths in yarny vomit. He says *yarny vomit* and opens his mouth wide over me.

I see where they took his tonsils out with ice cream. They put ice cream in the back and froze that part and then the tonsils just came out. That is what Bessie says. She is named after a cow and knows about how animals as well as people work because she was a nurse before nursing got to be too much work. So ice cream is what I see when his mouth is open like that. I am not scared. Besides, I know his talking isn't anything he can stop and so why be scared of it? When Mom switched me in with him, even though he is a boy and there isn't much room in the closet for dresses, I didn't think he would talk—but everyone should, I now think.

As for the dresses, he tore all the sashes out to make more room. But I didn't tell Mom. I sewed them and sewed them, all of them lined up like extra legs at the bottom of the closet, and holes where they were meant to be. He is not sorry. He can't make a bow, that's what I think, not anything about the dresses, which is what he says in the night.

Hear him talk now?

Days, he's so quiet, Mom's best boy, just not so good in work at school. His papers always get dirty and make wrinkles and wads in the sharp corners of everything he turns in. I'm the one who smoothes them and finds his place. I do this just before the light goes off and he starts to talk. No one can hear him, we are so far from Mom. The kitchen's in the way and the living room. We are at the end of the *L* they make, and the baby is closer. So when he makes his noises after I turn the light off, I could be in a place with real animals, the way it sounds, and who would know?

Mom says I should like to stay with him because he likes to take care of me. Also because there is a new baby for a while in my room. Mom also says one night he was standing in front of the stairs with me in his arms and telling me about the stairs and how I should stay off them. I was smaller then, arm-size. But I am not sure now whether he was warning me or wanting me to try the stairs. After all, he says other people should try the stairs. Which people I am not sure anymore because I don't know all the ones in his class he doesn't like because the people change every night.

I don't say anything about how he talks because he will grow out of it, the way the baby stopped screaming at the dog and now drinks his water. When he talks, he is changing. He is growing out of himself, is what I think.

Like those animals that leave their skin or eat it.

He is so tired in the morning I think he must be changing a lot. He can't even get his clothes on until I am gone to breakfast and he has left me some quarters. The quarters are for punching me. He loves quarters and to give them to me is hard. But I said it is not fair I should get punched. He says if he can punch me and not tell he will share them. I usually take only one quarter. Once I took three and he couldn't stop and ended up giving me all the quarters he had found that week. I am not good at finding them like he is.

He reads the encyclopedia after he turns the light back on, after he tells about who in the class and how they are bad to him that day especially, and how he would change it. When I hear A-for-Aardvark begin and the story of the earth pig and South America and the notes at the end that say further reading, more and more reading, I know I can start to sleep, although I know it's not over. He wakes me at G always because he's skipped some, he says he's sorry he skipped some, he'll have to start over, what about the punching?

Once he missed punching me and fell backwards off the bed, and had a nosebleed. I am the one who gathered the lot of tissues from however long it took him to stop the bleeding, and I took these tissues and flushed them so Bessie wouldn't find them and say the doctor will have to put a balloon up his nose to stop the blood like they did once when he was at school. This is why he is so pale that morning and why I yawn, this is why Mom gets after me with her question.

I am not bored, Mom, I say, but no more.

I don't usually talk.

These quarters I get are going to buy me a doll, a big doll, my size. I don't care if its limbs are all stiff, a kind of rock plastic, and the face is equal in plainness to mine. She can be beside me when he leaves.

And he will leave. Mom says all children leave—the sooner, the better.

Polio

If you play hide and seek in the dark, you won't get polio, said Mrs.

Then she went in. We slapped at bugs that liked the porch light until I turned it off and said, Let's watch TV instead.

You're it, said one and then the other from the porch corners. For talking.

I didn't count or close my eyes but they went away anyway. Except the littlest with her wet diapers. I carried her to base and put her down. Then I did this jig we had to know for the school musical and someone cleared his throat like he was waiting.

Game over, I shouted and climbed base, not a very big tree.

I hated babysitters worse than baby sisters, the one on the ground crying, wanting up. From where I was, I could see Mrs. with her legs crossed in front of the TV with a doctor show on and our bowl of popcorn half-snacked up. In six short years I could be Mrs. too. I had breasts, my shorts were that short, I knew about babies.

She's wet, I said, loud into the dark. You scared her, I have to take her in. I knew they wouldn't stay out without me, even if the boys said It, It to each other.

The sitter switched channels to news as soon as we settled. Bedtime, she said.

No. We have consensus, I said. I used the last word coming from the news.

We were moving toward the suitcases, the ones stacked in the corner with the winter clothes supposed to be soon turned to summer. She laughed at consensus and left with the baby.

Never, I said after her.

We unstacked the suitcases, threw out the clothes before Mrs. even found a diaper. The boys were quick as movie robbers. The littlest was already sitting in a trunk when she came back, the whole kit and caboodle pretty much empty. Mrs. shut it on him.

In the dark you won't get polio, she said, and picked up

the trunk and carried it to the door. It's fun said the boy after some silence, so anybody who could fit climbed into the others. Then there were six cases by the door and me holding the baby who said Click, click.

Okay, said Mrs. and went into the kitchen for some more of this you-know-what in a bottle she kept refilling with water after she poured some into a Coke.

I let everybody out since they wanted to switch, everybody but the last girl since the lock on that one stuck pretty much always. After a while, after we tried a bobby pin and then a nail and then a paper clip—or rather me, since the others had started watching TV—the lock finally came loose with Dad's hammer.

Mrs. came in with the new noise and said, Give me that baby, who, of course, wanted her own bottle and was crying. Then Mrs. couldn't find the nipple and the baby hated the cup which was still filled with what Mrs. had been having so she said, If you play chute you don't get polio either.

Chute? Or Shoot? We didn't know which until she'd wrapped the baby in some of the thick winter things lying around and tossed her down it.

At the bottom, in the basement, sat a huge mound of laundry, a lot of diapers mostly, so the baby, who was quite quiet for a while, Mrs.' intention, broke nothing. Of course then we all wanted a turn and I think one of the boys sprained his wrist but he knew better than to tell in front of Mrs. and went to bed right away, like the rest of us.

A consensus? asked Mrs. Then, in the dark, she told us a story about a house very much like ours that had someone walking around it and around it, putting his face in the windows, and then coming in, and he had polio.

What's this polio thing? It's boring, I said.

Nothing, said Mrs. Go to sleep, she said and snapped her gum that she wouldn't share with us but that Dad had left us. Nothing, but my brother has it, said Mrs. Then she breathed in all our faces and said, Don't let the bugs bite.

Mom, I said in the morning. Besides, she wouldn't give us the gum.

Mom laughed. You know how many sitters would sit with all of you, or at what price? Anyway, I've heard she's going to have one of her own. What could be better?

Cave Life

WE WERE NEANDERTHAL, our cave icebound Canada, a basement apartment. Our Neanderthal love we expelled with grunts in white vapors, the kind of unwavering, always-lit lust that passes for passion if you are too Neanderthal to know better.

Our cave closed by the start of October under the shirr of serious snow, the half-earthed windows aglow with the first week's mornings of new fill, then dark and more dark under the shutter of the next six million flakes. Our front door wouldn't open by the second week, the door that exited onto the garden we thought so September-beautiful was soon bowed with snow chest-high.

Reduced rent was what the parlor floor got in exchange

for letting everyone in the building roll through their window onto their bed, where they liked the light, though everyone entered snow-dusted or iced, and at any hour, often with them in it. Two short taps and a long, and either the Florida flamenco guitarist our age answered, whose sideburns—the very word for these Dylanesque growths suggested the fierce heat that kept luring the other parlor floor occupant, an older, pillowy Greek girl, back onto his mattress for another roll—or she did, appearing with kimono akimbo. Only she could shove it open. He would only flash his long fingernails at us saying Sorry while we shivered. How the Greek girl endured his stroking we couldn't imagine, stroking each other in absent lust while our bologna roasted or our cabbage fiesta married. Upstairs they never quit, her heels breaking into a thumping flamenco halfway across the floor, our ceiling heaving. Our thumping back she answered with her feet, picking up our rhythm, mocking us, making us smile, until, in a single fast pass, the bed sang back in a sudden silence. He called her his Rabbit. He was Dog. Dog, dog, dog, we heard shouted out of that silence. And then more flamenco: she would slip her shoes back on, fall to the floor in another volatile series of heel poundings.

Were they any good? We'd only heard them. Invited once to drink the raspberry wine we thought the best kind you could buy, they danced for us, and her fleshy dark heaviness made its point, as did his nails flashing to every toss of her head. More Spanish than anyone Spanish, they did dance for money somewhere suburban.

But what they knew best was not flamenco but fighting. Our battles mewed and spent themselves in shivering kisses while theirs raged and broke with chords crashing, the sound of kitchenware methodically coming off the walls, each pot heavier than the last, its landing against the dull sheet-rock a profound, slightly higher-toned thud, almost flamenco in rythm. More than once did she fling open the window spitting Greek invective over her shoulder, while he smoked in a far corner, ash dropping to his bare chest, smoked and ignored all of us. Dog? he said. Bitch.

Then he went on tour without her, and she came and sat on our floor—we had no chairs—and wept for loneliness, sang Janis Joplin in Greek, wrung her peasant skirt, a real peasant skirt, and finished off all our wine herself. She led us upstairs—you patting her bum as it rose in front of you on the step—where she kept retsina under her bed. Soon we were all toasting the snowman who had appeared next to the stoop outside her window a week earlier. He wore a hat that we'd found blowing down the street, and the day before I'd given him my cracked rubber boots, screwed them into the sides as arms. After we finished off that bottle, we crawled through her window and wedged in the empty upwards at the groin, to make him, as you said, more snow-manly. By then she was asleep and we had to pry her window back open with the tip of your boot, one foot dancing. She only sighed as we lunged over her bed, laughing out steam and hot under our threadbare clothes.

Days later the thaw started, and after we came through her window with wet boots once, we had to shovel ourselves out and go in through our own door. It took another week before the highest drifts softened and the retsina bottle fell and my boots began to droop and we found him.

The police had to jackhammer him up. They could have waited one more day for another inch of melt but no one in the crowds who gathered at our stoop really wanted to walk past someone wrapped like some garden statue or wintering sapling the way the police had at first left him. One of his fingers vibrated off with the jackhammering, the finger with the longest guitar claw. I saw the chief pocket it—well, slide it into a bag. But they didn't really need clues—if a finger could be called a clue—because she embraced the police the minute she answered the door. She had called them herself after I told her I thought I saw one of his shoes sticking out from the snow where she'd just repacked it. We'd made lewd jokes about her bent down in front of him.

She said he'd walked out without a coat on, swearing his heat would hold him for as long as it took her to cool off. Equally furious, she'd gone to bed, expecting him to tap submissively on the window at any moment. A snowy wind shrieked and fell in piles for an hour. They were warm weather people, they didn't know snow. She opened the window and waited, a drift piling up on the bed around her. In the early morning, when the wind had died down, he was there, she said, stiff, snow like a rug thick all over him. She couldn't haul him in. Seeing drunks heaving a big ball down the middle of the street, she ran out and packed more snow around him, in three big bulges. Then she told us he'd gone on tour.

The papers called it an accident and she didn't move away, she played flamenco records and stamped and stamped until our lights went out, and wore the customary black, surely sweaty in the ensuing summer nights. She often sat at her window and stared. She must have become used to staring that winter.

At the first hint of cold, two leaves dropping, we moved and moved, especially to places with sun and very little snow. We also learned to fight. Club or be clubbed was what finally tapped into us as we huddled beside our dark snow-filled windows that previous winter. Now sex didn't make a resounding Yes to all our No's, the no lunch, no heat, no lights, no gas, the no fun life we lived. We went in and out of our own doors and no amount of tapping, short or long, could open anything. And one day you didn't come back and I stood there, rooted, and never knew how cold I had become, how inescapably cold, until someone else noticed.

Psychic

THE AUNT DOESN'T WANT TO show me the shoe. It's too much like you're a dog, she says.

That's okay, I say. I'd like to take another look at the snapshots.

As the sister flips through the album for the place, the boyfriend says, no, no—wait a minute, here's how she signed herself, and he pulls out a scrap of paper ripped off a letter with Love still stuck to it.

Both the aunt and the sister rear back like the corpse is still curling the *e*.

Can you see it? he asks.

Smooth it out, I say.

He does.

I don't like the look of his hands. Not one bit. Too happy with themselves. I smooth out the paper myself, over and over.

This is getting expensive, says the aunt who lifts her feet from side to side while she waits. Remember, she's by the hour.

I turn over the signature. It's a signal to myself. Mrs., I say. Don't fret.

If it was an accident, wouldn't we know by now? whines the sister. They always find the car wrecked somewhere, right? Maybe she's still alive and ran off.

It wasn't an accident, says the aunt. And she is not alive.

Oh, great, let's not get into this again, says the boyfriend.

I can have my ideas, says the aunt. I might be right. She nods to me. You don't go missing this long—

Shut up, shut up, says the sister, holding her hands to her ears.

If you want, you two can step outside, I say. It might help me concentrate.

The man is bigger alone. So are those hands that hang from his sleeves by his sides, that curl and stay curled.

I can't help you, I say right away.

Ma'am?

What I mean is, she's not alive. That's all. Where she is is another matter entirely.

He looks at his watch.

Yes, I do charge by the hour, otherwise people call me day and night, I say.

So you know where she is, says the boyfriend.

I nod. I hand back the signature.

He leaves it on the table between us. That's great, he says. Just great.

He does not look at me.

Don't you want to know where?

Sure, of course, he says. That's what we're paying you so much for. He puts those hands in his pockets, he takes them out again. I turn away and touch the map where I know she is. Call the ladies in. Let me tell everybody at once.

He doesn't move. Maybe I should break it to them myself, he says. It's easier that way. They pretty much think she's not gone.

I touch the spot again. All right, I say. Whatever. But I'd like to be paid now. People go off and find the body and then suddenly change their minds about my fee. In fact, usually I take all the money up front.

Why'd you make us an exception? He is reaching into his pocket now, sounding gruff.

A feeling, I say. I'm psychic.

He pretends to laugh. He lays a checkbook onto the table. He writes in my fee, then extra.

I don't say it's too much.

Now you could look in the river, by the bend, is what I say. If you wanted. And you could check in the quarry five miles further. That's where the other shoe is.

He is carefully penning in the size of the check into his ledger while I talk, and he is finished only when he's rewritten the figure wrong twice. Why, thank you, he says, for the option.

Want to ask me anything else?

He looks at me. Asking is the last thing on his mind.

Well, let them in, I say.

The women are stomping on my mat. He unlocks the catch and they burst through the door with nervous laughs, the only kind people make around me. We figured you must've soul-searched to heaven by now, says the sister.

Hush, says the nervous aunt, taking one of her gloves off, hush.

I am finished, I say.

The boyfriend and I look at each other.

It's no use, says the boyfriend. Let's get out of here, he says, taking the aunt's elbow, steering the sister out the door. It was truly the absolute waste of time I thought it would be. You dragged me all the way out here for nothing.

I don't contradict him. I watch them go, the flustered sister, the slow aunt. The aunt is slow in disappointment and quite angry. I hear her ask whether he paid me, and his answer.

I turn back to tidy the cups and see he's forgotten the slip with the signature. I slide it into a drawer where I might find it later, when he comes back.

He will come back.

Electricity

THE SPACE ABOVE THE ground, way above, and over the grain bin, all over, is full of air but also full of wires. He doesn't think about wires, plunging a pole into the bin where the stuck grain sits. He thinks *pro-bin*, get that grain to settle into it. He doesn't think about fall. Even the sway of the ladder so many feet up puts more shove into him, not grab. He swings the pole up and out into all that air to get more jab—and he catches. That is, the wires catch the pole and in that kind of catch—that long, long catch—you fall.

Now, the thing about electricity is its exit. You may think that a jolt of that power—those are real wires, not just lines, the ones that clear the bin entirely, fling you through that great deal of air from high up to down, and leave a hefty stigmata on both palms where the pole touches—is enough. But no. Electricity wants earth. So when the hand that holds the rod holds the current, in that thrilling moment when the sky offers its lit butt, the volts don't squirm or relax or break off but thrust right through a person, then out his hind end to where its straight line wants to stop, to bury itself.

To bury.

It is no seizure. He has had seizures galore and this is not one of them, this pop-branching inside his head and down is not this. He has that thought and then more in the first few minutes of recline on his fractured back, waiting for anyone.

Not that anyone is there.

He is stubborn and alone, as always.

He tries not to look at his hands but there they are, and raw. He doesn't want to look at the wires, but they jitter and swing overhead, all in the motion of fun. Except for his back, he would have grabbed the pole and beaten them silly, and then beat at the bin because the bin had lured him up. Beating is what you want to do back, to anybody and -thing. Except for the burn on his hind end and his hands. Except for his back. Instead, after the snout of those volts finishes nosing him, both sides, he crawls to the shed to the phone and skips 911, goes for the zero. Fourteen times he tries zero. You think about a lot, he thinks, a lot about zero when you are fried and can't dial.

Then he faints.

Over gravel like that, you can miss the turn off or first left or first right. The volunteers drive past two sections, then put on the siren and drive faster past the—to them—featureless fields, until they reverse, until they drive right up. Splints and tape will fix him, they say, but they can't splint the in and out of current, no unguent they have will do it, no juice for the fever that spikes with it. They strap him into a plane just big enough for a gurney, and a pilot takes him, jolting—ground, ground, air—somewhere better.

You wouldn't think his parents at a party would think twice. The party is a reunion besides, people they see every five years and not between. But the parents have their lives: he is almost forty. And it isn't as if this is his first accident, no, it is a Wolf he has cried too often. All those seizure problems—this time it is just electricity. Of course he is fine, they say. They stand shaking their heads over Scotch and talking of specialists, about how electricity goes away, it isn't a car body wrapped around a tree that has to be towed, or blood in a bathtub, or a finger lost on a freeway that needs sewing.

Even the phone service is okay or he couldn't have dialed out, says the father.

Intensive care? ask his siblings as if it is something they are afraid to purchase. They shuffle in, trailing their own emergencies—wives who aren't speaking, kids who fall on the front step and get nosebleeds. They spend their waiting time asking, Does electricity fry everything on the way—

flank steak to flank steak? Or, Remember the embassy in Russia that got cooked in the Cold War? Yes, it was rays but what else is electricity? Talk like that carries, covers up the Wolf business that makes them feel foolish replacing the parents. But not too.

Besides pity, they have twin-fear, that he is them and they might languish with the same business. And they love him. The way a mate is dispensable, he is not. After all, he is their brother. And he is good, the way goodness is a collection of symptoms. They list when and why but not too much or they could jinx him, so they pretend he is just their brother and no bother.

What the nurses are saying is, He's talking, they who don't know how odd it is that this brother should talk, this brother who uses words in abeyance, in extremis. In this family speaking is dangerous. A line must be open and all the incoming current is streaming out through his mouth. Unless the nurses meant screaming. This is, after all, the Midwest, where the nurses say, Excuse me, I have some kind of emergency, as if it is UPS with a package they must sign for.

In Intensive Care you can't get better than Satisfactory. Excellent goes elsewhere. Now exactly how soon to Satisfactory? his siblings are asking.

The doctors lick their lips.

They don't ask, Die? They ask, How will you change this, with drugs or cuts?

The doctors brighten. The doctors touch their finger whorls, they say, We will move skin tomorrow, from here to here, they say, until it's very Satisfactory.

The nurses say, Excuse me, Emergency.

He looks happy from the this and this. Well, let's wait and see, say the doctors. Let's have him walk first. Let him learn that first. There is nothing for the siblings to do but watch him lean into the IV and spot his feet the way a ballerina does twirling, and not cry. This he does for three days, three days of spots while the siblings are waiting for the parents. It is all right they say, weighing their own children, for a parent to be finished being a parent. But they look at the toys on the floor, they look away. Then one brother breaks down and says, What about me? The wives close around him.

When the parents come, the siblings kiss them back from alumnae and say how close this accident was and ask if there is anything else they can do and then leave. After all, the parents are his family and not the siblings with their own, who teach their own to walk in the foyer. He says as they go, There is nothing like electricity to bring a family together.

But the parents don't stay. This time they go home quickly and let him move to a motel to save hospital space. In this space recommended, of course, by doctors, once a day a nurse comes and checks his skin, or almost once a day. It is in this space where he lies with *Star Trek* and news and does not dial zero again and again, but waits.

The wait is for a hot tub in the outdoors over current, but home. It is from this tub he heaves, from the wet hot into the dry cold, his back clenching and unclenching. He climbs out and goes for the door and leaves a pheasant to drain in the snow in a blue shadow in the dark of the tub and its hot.

Never would he leave a pheasant outside drained, for there are cats. He leaves it now with ice on his nose, leaves it with a swing swinging behind him for no reason but his knocking it in his hurry.

Electricity plays under the hot tub, hotting up the mist that trails him as he leaves, as he lurches in. Electricity chases him: you can see it in the mist, you can see it (if you could) in his head, branching and blooming as he hurries, having seizures. What you do see is the branch the swing is hung on, all of it pointing at the pheasant, bird-curled in blue shadow at the tub base. This place where the pheasant and the branching come together is where he suffers an exchange at the base where the neck hits the head in coaxial knot. Yes, electricity seizes him in the head: where once it leapt in neuron up and down, it now unknots and branches throughout, pure synapse snapping.

Nonetheless, there's the phone. He makes as if to dial—was he thinking of zero?—and it falls off its cradle.

The father finds the cradle in the morning. It is found

then, as if lost. But this time those who come after find him easily, though they are wrapping holiday presents and sanding last-minute initials when the *ooga* sounds, when they take their places.

He wears no clothes from the tub so they wrap him. The father finds the clothes but just holds them. Maybe the father has a gene that lights off the charge, maybe the act of making him set it off? And the mother? She has her genes. When was he last us? she is asking. Who did we have?

Nurses from before, from the motel and elsewhere, and women who took his temperature when no one else wanted it, maybe to impress their dates or test the alarm on the instrument, sign their names in a book in the room where he lies. They sign and sign until the man in black sitting in the rear clears his throat.

Alone as always, says the sound.

Then the siblings, with their children who say, I don't like this, come three on a side. Hush, say the siblings as they walk, but only into the cold. They pass the doctor who overcharged for the electrocution, whose bills lie around the phone in piles upon which he lay so stiff without clothes the father knew at once but said otherwise when he phoned the mother who phoned the volunteers—the doctor comes, for those bills are paid.

Patrolmen take off their hats and stop traffic in two places while he rides by, while a charge gathers in the air above him, in clouds now. But there is no down in that space where he is going, where he can't fall, the space between the ground and his head close and quiet.

One of the siblings must speak and comfort, say the father and mother. Words run up and down inside this one in electric horror-movie hurry, but they are not their words. They are his. And he needs no comfort.

But the charge is still there, and they can feel it. This sibling looks over the air and its charge, where it gathers, where it leans, and this one says:

No one replaces the parents.

Petrified Woman

WHO PAID FOR THE CRANE to hoist her out? The town, a circus, a syndicate? The glass case contained the least of what there was, the coffin husked, the coffin far lighter than the stone body with its marks of the soul in struggle, its flesh turning to rock in the dark, its face all charred, a face that had been dragged hellward and spat out.

In Japan a woman like this would be displayed in a department store, not a library. Her mother had taken her to Japan when she was young. She had seen a meteorite in such a store, faintly glowing in its own glass case. Even then, the display surprised her. Didn't the Japanese fear anything that glowed? But people are attracted to their fears.

She touched the woman. Rather, she touched the glass near the woman's face. The effort and its frustration canceled each other out and she liked that. That no bell sounded after reassured her that it was okay to touch and not touch, that she could do it again. She dotted the case with prints.

The card stopped her. She read it through, all about the woman's when and where and what. She had read it before, many times, but never with such leisure. Now she had time to think twice, and didn't.

The window on her left showed an old man strolling toward a streetlight far enough away. It was dead night, the sky the color of the woman's face, and it was the library, the tomb of the town even on an Amnesty Afternoon for fines. The librarian used oxygen when she had to reshelve, she was that old, and the hissing of the tank made her deaf.

Not that the librarian was around to hear.

She swung her hammer down hard. Glass bounced off her hands, caught in her hair. She skittered to a corner. With all that staring at the woman, the glass had disappeared, she'd forgotten about the glass. But now only the rock remained, and that was what she went back for, with the hammer.

After so many blows, all you could recognize was the nose. She pocketed it and the card from the case. Crumbly petrified bits had bounced off the chairs, across the open *O.E.D.*, against the window. The larger chunks had settled on top of poetry.

She put the hammer deep into her handbag and began screaming.

The strolling old man stopped lifting his key to the apartment adjacent.

She screamed louder.

He dropped his keys and took those few steps over to the library door and wrenched it open, the one on the left that she had jimmied herself. She sobbed when he took her by the shoulders. Miss Kratowsky!

She sobbed louder and pointed.

Oh, dear, he said. Was there an explosion?

She nodded into her kerchief to keep herself from laughing. His face!

He called 911 and the librarian. While they waited, the summer night air hung under the sudden fluorescence that the old man had switched on, filling the empty sorting shelves with a cold that prompted her to talk rather than stare into its bright flicker.

She told him about the vandal, tall and Germanic—just like everybody around here—who had wielded a heavy date stamp coming out of the library just as she had rounded the corner on her way home from fetching aspirin for her mother.

He ran south. She didn't hear a car.

The librarian burst into real wailing as soon as she arrived and saw what the cop was sweeping up. We had to get a grant to hang on to the damn thing. Everett Library wanted it. Now they'll just say I dropped it.

Now, now, said the cop. It would take more than a dropping to do all this. He bent over to pick up a needle-sized black shard.

Fingerprints, said the librarian.

Smacked like this? I doubt it. But he tossed the shard in a bag just the same.

She fingered the nose in her purse, then her hammer, a cool weight at the bottom. Will you drop me? she asked the cop. She had told her story exactly the same three times and she couldn't do it again or she'd have to start changing things. You couldn't repeat too much right.

Sorry about the mess, he said, hauling out an armful of papers and loose chip bags so she could slide in. I just got no place to put all this. He wedged the trash back in at her side until she was pressed right up next to him like a high school date. What would he say if she said she had touched the man who ran off?

I would think you were some kind of old lady, he said, making an animal shimmy with her so close. Go on—you could have hit him over the head with that handbag of yours and been a hero. A big handbag like that, he said, and almost patted it.

Officer, she said. Keep your hands to yourself. Then quick enough they were at her door. She exited with a trail of paper and plastic that he clutched for as she slammed the door.

Somebody had left the TV on. She ought to live alone. She banged open the door and walked past the TV topped with the salt and pepper shakers that somebody had bought in Japan because no one there used salt and pepper, and she went straight to the kitchen and dug a hole in the flowerpot on the sill.

The nose fit fine. She patted and watered it.

I thought you were watching that, she shouted to the somebody sitting up in bed. I am going to have to stop paying for cable if you don't watch it when it's on, she said. At least I'm going to watch my own programs.

The old woman put on her slippers and came into the kitchen where the girl was suddenly crying, hanging over the sink with sobs.

That won't do you a bit of good, said the old woman. I've got a heart of stone and you know it. Where's my aspirin?

She pointed at her purse. The old woman dumped the contents, found what she needed and left, dragging her slippers forward.

She wiped her tears away with tissue spilled from her handbag. The card from the case lay under a tube of lipstick. She read it again. The trees swayed in the dark and some strange bird moaned while she read by the light of the TV that it was only the mother who turned to stone, not the child, that the child was spared.

Leadership

YOU STRIKE ME AS A leader, says his father.

The boy turns his face—because the rest of him is being suited—toward his father raising buttered toast. What kind of leader?

He's teasing, sighs the mother who pats the boy down, extracting the dollar he got for switching line leader with a bigger boy, a much bigger boy, moving it from a pocket into an envelope. You *could* be a leader, she says and puts that bigger boy's name on the outside of the envelope and pockets it herself.

Both the boy and father hear how she puts the *could,* but the boy does not care other than that is his dollar she has sealed up and tucked on her person, at least as far as he's concerned, and he is not going to show her any of those other dollars or anymore that he gets if this is it, if this is how it is. Leading is not what he wants anyway. You get shoved from behind if you lead, you have to know which door. And if you talk, you have to go to the back of the line, but the rest of them talk, yes they do.

A robin has set down in the too short grass and its rear end twitches like it tickles. The grass is too short like the truth she's putting out, grass that he could cut himself on, it is so sharp that short.

Eat your breakfast, she says to him who is so solemn with his empty pocket, sure she will look in another. He cranes his neck more toward the window.

A rocket has landed beside the robin. It is the size of a small dog and it appears to have legs that it is stretching like it has finished a long trip. It's a what? he asks. On the grass.

Hush, she says. I see.

What are we going to do about it? she says. You—have a look.

His father drops his toast and his napkin upends on his knee as he too stands. Then the two males look at each other, one knowing the value of saying nothing, the other the value of looking away, of seeing nothing. You have to be careful, the father says, and the word *careful* rises in a bubble, getting bigger and bigger until the father could walk inside it like some future vehicle, like the answer vehicle to the one that is so improbably running beside the harried robin.

I saw somewhere that tomatoes are being grafted onto some important part of a chicken, you know, something small that doesn't count as a chicken, he says.

The mother and the son do not turn toward him, do not *hmmm.* The mother feels for the knob on the radio, for the comfort of emergency broadcast.

The boy, however, has a gun. It's in a place his mother hasn't felt. So what if it's a toy. What it is is another bribe from the bigger boy, a real fake gun. He unlatches the door.

Get back in here, she says.

He walks into the prickly grass, holding the gun above his bellybutton and out. The rocketship stops running all over the yard and comes over and sort of sniffs his pants. The boy wants to say Good Boy but he doesn't, he fires away because he has this real fake thing in his hands.

The father comes up behind him. Furthest away the mother halts. They look up. The sky is going all slatey like in a painting people say is important. In the second they take to glance up, the rocketship retracts its legs and tail and plays dead.

Whether the weather, that sudden cover of sun, is part of the rocketship's strategy is not clear, but if the spiritual is at the bottom of what you believe and you believe the spiritual is not of this earth, then of course the rocketship could control the physical. It's now all foggy or that's what the mother swears later when she points at the rocketship on the shelf in her son's room for the cameras. But just then, the three of them in a line near this rocketship deployed yet solemnly quiet, they don't say much at all. Martha, the father murmurs as he has never murmured before, not even at night, Martha, hold my hand.

The boy wouldn't have answered to anything if anyone had asked. He throws himself to his knees and touches the rocketship because he knows what it wants: Take me to your leader. He is obeying, he is scooping it up in his arms, opening and closing all the little portholes. The bigger boy will let him in line now.

Sweetheart, says his mother, Give me that now.

Party Girl

THE MOVIE SPEEDS ALONG. She and he and the Wolfman, or It, or giant ants. No sound. Who can hear with the snoring, the scraping, the mechanical clicks and stops of dialing up boys? The party is going well when the party girl says over it: They get divorces.

The twins start to giggle then, taking turns. Divorces? they cry. Divorces! They laugh so hard they really cry but who knows the joke? All the party girl said was what happens to TV stars when they have to kiss other people. The party girl blinks. Then smiles. They have a mother with a divorce so they think they know. But it is her party and her mother who lets them mess up the bathroom with hair gel, who lets them flick on and off the TV. Let them kiss other people, let them double-kiss the TV.

Her TV has a long cord that reaches up into the basement half-window, creating a draft, a finger of cold that gets down into her sleeping bag by her leg. The TV cord barely makes it to the kitchen outlet. You can see it strung out across the linoleum if you go upstairs. Once already Shirley has unplugged it going on her first trip to the bathroom, and now the father, stumbling, has backed out Wolfman into static which they have to fix.

The party girl feels her breasts. They are talking cup now, what old women wear under housedresses. She is in another country where you could wear just grass on a string around your middle forever. What would Tarzan think? He would get used to it. I would probably fit a double A coconut, she says out loud, but the others are looking at their fingernails now, and on the screen someone is kissing again, this time the absolute wrong person.

The party girl wiggles further into her bag. Getting kissed by the wrong person—how can you tell for sure? She smells the heat in her bag. Now that she showers every day, she has forgotten the smell. She is an animal like the screen couple, their legs cramped from sitting so close together in the front seat, captured and tortured by the It and getting older with more smell.

If she digs into her bag so only one eye can get cold and the rest boils, she is safe. But Shirley sticks a receiver against her arm in the bag, with a boy talking on it. Dead mouse, dead mouse, screeches Shirley, and she pulls it out by the cord and her fingertips like it bites, and the boy is still talking.

No one sleeps. The party girl gets out of her bag and eats more cake. It looks green in the absolute dark but with red spots where the seance candles puddle over their holders. No ghost hangs around however. All they got was a squeak in the chair the party girl is sitting on. Not like at the other party where the ouji wouldn't stay still, where they had the phone play on the board by itself.

The moon is finished, like the cake now. It is strange to see it gone. She is about to say something moony when Shirley does the Heimlich maneuver on one of the party girl's big dolls, saying how you have to know this to be a waitress which is what she wants to be.

Now the girls dance, now they jump rope. Now they all stand still for the National Anthem, and prop up Becky who will not wake up but just smiles, because she has to do her brother's paper route when it gets light. Then the twins hyperventilate and fall down. Then the screen is snowing like everything is over.

Ah, to be eleven again, the party girl says, lighting the seance candlestubs with the lighter. The lighter comes from the emergency pack her mother is saving for when the bomb drops, she says. None of the other girls say anything. They just dial, this time to the boys' grandmothers and then to hang up after they ask, Do you know where Bert or Rodney is? and giggle.

Jammed up to her pillow is an album cover with two people looking at a moon, but not the one that people walk on because it is so close in their convertible that it seems to keep them apart. At that cover moon the twins are tossing giggle poison now, popcorn, tossing it and letting it roll into Becky's open mouth after the cover bounce.

Someone is going to the bathroom now because she can hear her mother shout out across the living room upstairs What time is it? like she, the girl, is a burglar. At school they heard the story about the party where a parent shot a girl climbing in the window after talking to some boys. They thought she was the same one the week before who took the set, the silver, and the trophies. It was the father's hunting rifle next to the bed just in case, they said.

That's why the party girl asks her father, when she's coming out of the bathroom and he's at the fridge, whether he has ever hunted. After he pours in milk with the grapeshot—Grapenuts is too personal, he says—what he says is, Hunting? Me? No, but your brother can't find his lizard.

Her brother comes down to tell everyone it is loose, her mother said to. So? say the twins together with Shirley. We like lizards, and they lean toward him saying he is cute and would he like to protect them? The brother doesn't stay and the party girl knows he is really worried about that lizard. He paid for it with his own money. The girls think he put it in the toilet which is why they're all going upstairs, even though the party girl says lizards don't like water that much. Not that he wouldn't try it, she says, and yawns.

Usually when the party girl falls asleep, the curlers against her skull are just like the pillow. Now she has a half-dream about being one of those guys who lie around on a board full of nails sticking up, and then Indian tortures of things going under the nails, the ones the nuns read at rest time last year to keep the boys quiet. Shirley has already pulled out her curlers, but she is naturally curly. At twelve, what will it be in hair for the party girl? More curls? More parts? You need a fortuneteller for fashion. But nobody fell for the party girl's mother's palm readings. Who is tall and dark in seventh grade? Girls. The party girl is the tallest.

But the party is a success because she finds out where to get nylons without a mother. Shirley has a catalogue that will send even bras in a plain wrapper. That makes her feel safe. She can't buy them in a store or someone will see and tell, and she says No to shoplifting, not like the twins.

So far a success. And there is not much left to change that. The morning is coming. She sees it through the half-window and she sees then, all at once, that this, and not when someone jumps out from behind the fridge and stops your heart, is what it is to be dead: the snowy set light, the no moon and dull stars and almost sun but not, the sound upstairs so far away it could be a pharaoh's pots and pans, and the smell of bacon that makes you so hungry you have to shut your eyes.

A Mama

MORNINGS, IT'S THE SAME. Break in, search the place, take the kid and some kid's clothes and dress him. Then off to the home. And every morning, the parent or parents lock the doors and/or hide in the coat closet and/or claw and kick at me while I pry away their kid. Their kid that is probably cut or bruised or burnt from anything, even a hot comb—every so often I see it, some regular ridges, and the parent saying he fell against a radiator. A lot of radiator action in these places.

So the court says take them. The court says take them and then bring them back every day at night because we can't keep them. The law. See, just because you want to kill a kid doesn't mean you're not entitled to free daycare.

I don't get it.

But they pay me. So I get them every morning, my partner and I, my partner who sits in the car waiting just in case. It's harder than you think, going in and getting little ones just born and bigger, big enough they get mean like their folks. But it's really the folks that are the problem. It's not like the kids don't want to go. No, two meals a day and somebody to cry to—that's the life for them. They're not going to mess that up.

Why, this one I got in the car here already barely moves its legs, this one, and every day I can see in the eyes why. So I don't get too attached. Get attached and they'll weep all over you every night and beg not to go home, and I've seen grown-up executives who volunteer and break down and bawl when they start begging and then the schedule gets all screwed up and I have to drive back late. I got a life too.

The kids will eat yours up.

I got my own kids. My own kids cry. When they do, I wallop them, but not hard, not hard like these do. These other parents, well, they go too far in the discipline department. Sometimes a little straightening out is good, kids appreciate it. But you have to realize that they do not like it to death or every day or when you just feel like it. These kids, for instance, I can't lay a hand on even if they beg for it.

The law.

For this one I beat at the door until the key drops down, I go into the bathroom where I know this joker likes to hide them. I turn off the hot water that steams up the place and the kid is bright red but no burns. Good. I take it into the bedroom where there's clothes, or if not, a blanket.

There's nothing in there but rags.

A ton of rags, and nothing too clean. I got extra blankets in the van anyway. I put the kid, who's not too hot anymore, into my jacket and head out.

But this parent makes me nervous. This one is not a first offender. This one last week put the kid in a sling over the door so it would drop on my head when I opened it. I am wary. I go quick for the knob.

This is where they always turn up, if they are not totally out of it. This is when parents stand around like they want to do something and slow me up and, of course, make the kid cry. This one's been crying Mama for some time and then screaming and then quiet. And, sure enough, there the parent is. When it sees the parent it's quiet again, this one, and it buries its—what do you think?—eighteen-month-old head in my chest and practically stops breathing.

This parent smiles like it is normal, like it is going to receive a nice kiss and a wave. See this smile? is what this parent's face says. I whip out a pen for the signature on the form as a sort of defense. I bring this form daily, the one that says I took the kid, checked it out like a book, and that I promise to bring it back later, because this usually takes their mind off me when they start to scare me.

But not this one. The parent gives a big kiss to the baby's neck and I am afraid for the baby when I see the big red lips left there. We get out as soon as the parent signs, though I see by the outfit there's going to be more to pick up in some months.

It says Mama.

That's me. And there is some point when I feel okay about a Mama but that point is not always when it says it. Anyway a Mama is what it makes into the spread when it turns my way, all upset in its rags.

Rags is what I put it in, if it deserves them. Does it deserve them? Maybe no. This one I haven't hurt for a long time, and I mean time stretched out, gum-like time. See, there's no blood, not even a Band-Aid, no water from a lot of tears. Still, I am surprised that it turns and says what it says.

For a treat at light, I let it rock in the car seat which I like to place on the table where the roast would sit, its small leg dangling over cereal.

It usually cries what sounds like, Where are you going? when I step out of the room. Or, What about me? Today is not the same, it is, Hurry—I think. I think this one is too young for grudges.

But I experiment. You are given children when they are too small, but if you wait, your chance is up for experiment. For now, it fits good inside the car seat on the table and says nothing if I leave the room, even when I put on salt.

This disappoints me. Salt should get a sound out of it. I make some new redness and give it more salt. They say salt is antiseptic, that salt cleans. And lets you know it.

From now on, when I make more, I'll pick them up later, you know—board them. The hospital has this service that I saw at checkout—the place where they clip off the bracelets when the insurance looks good enough—where a few boarders in gray beds, no special tubes, no lights, lay around, looking up, nobody's. You know they'll take to you quick, no problem. You could even pick up spares. There was one girl standing around who wasn't even a nurse, just acted church-like in the way she looked at the boarders. She was just waiting for a turn at the rocker with one of those, and I saw she could be me, I could do that. I could come by later and say, What a baby this is, whose is it? and just pick it up. This would be a lot easier than having one come down the canal. That is a lot of bother, plus screaming. And you feel lousy tired for weeks after. Giving you reason. Good reason. They try not to tell you this at these classes. I guess they figure it will be Love at First Sight when it squeezes out. I must say love is not the first feeling I have, after. Not to mention how all my hair falls out six weeks later.

In all the classes I help at, there aren't more than five who really want one. I can see this in their eyes when they are breathing fast, all puffing and puffing, that they want a new car the same way. If they just spent a good week together with one, night as well as day, they would quit and not puff again and get out. But most of them hire someone to take over and so never do night plus day, just once in a while an afternoon. So the only hard part is the puffing and a little at the end.

I could also follow the ones with the cloudy wanting and wait. Some would not notice. Really. They are too tired with their new arrangements, their painting the broom closet blue and finding out about diapers that can be collected, their considering canceling whole seasons since they might be busy.

Before the hair falls out, always before then, you must start with the experiments. Otherwise, it will make such a crease in its face, a smile, from gas or whatever, that there's no moment right again for getting even. I give them up then if I miss. Why not? Too soon they talk, they say and point Mama. Like, for example, last night.

The screen door bangs. I think first, Fix it, then I think, this is a person, knocking. You could think the person wanted in, you could think, Open up in there. I take it into the bathroom, the room without a window, and turn on the hot and leave it. I go into the bedroom and still I hear that screen door. What a lot of noise, it and the screen door and the someone. I move to the place behind the door.

Someone will come and say, What's the problem? like they do every day, screen door or window or front door knocker.

And I'll say I'm just the sitter. I haven't seen the parents for days. I'm a sitter and I'm not supposed to open the door. They will look at me and my old teenage hair and face and believe me.

I'm the girl, grown. When I look at the bathroom mirror, I see the parent's face. I ask it often, How did it get there with its Mama all over it? I have scars that show my face should be the face of anyone else, not the reflection, not the face in the shininess of those scars that match.

My boyfriend says so too. He is the one who dips into me when there is an occasion, who says he will be Parent like he means it. Someday. On my birfday, he says, pretending to be a baby to get a baby. But I say, This is early, I say, Let's you and me play baby for us, together, on your birfday. I will sit deep in the beanbag chair, sit lolling, and you will—

He knows how this is supposed to go. I try this often. Often I need to do this, not just on his birfday, and him too, he likes it. What he does is he picks me up and holds me, with my limpness dripping my head and legs and arms all over his arms. He holds me in his white clothes, the ones he wears every day for the work he does with me, and he puts his big hand on my hair and moves it toward my face, slow, then lifts, and then moves. About halfway I make sounds. But I am only allowed to make small sounds like you hear in dogs when they sleep, and never a Mama.

Car Frogs

A MATTRESS TAKES UP MOST of the inside of the car in which I lie, watching stars thick as B-B shot against the windshield. Until my feet wedge in tighter, the steering wheel puts a kink in the overall comfort quotient, but wedging is how I get to be leaning on the handle, cloudburst weeping, when the door opens. I slip head down then, toward the short tennis shoes that shod the handle holder.

Nelson, I say, which is not a greeting.

I say to him, I am just figuring out a camping position.

I get up.

I thought you were sad, says Nelson. He is sad. I should know, he's the oldest of mine, he's been around the longest.

I brush my eyes with my hand. I say, Allergies. I fake sneeze. You want in?

He climbs in. He is round and soft and takes up too much room. We thrash into the canned fish position. Once there was a car, he starts, as if this is bed.

I shush him. The footsteps of dog walkers and concomitant jangly collars approach outside. The windows are so fogged already, the stars and not me weep as they pass.

In the shush, I pretend to fall asleep, I loosen my muscles from toes to collar to forehead wrinkle. I almost snore but I know that kind of snoring gives fake sleep away. The boy does his best with the brute night behind the stars and my deceit. He rolls and wriggles and whispers, We're on the ocean.

No one will find us if we drown, I could say. My eyes fill up, the pump of sadness registers, but after he quiets in this silence that we make together, he chews his lip and breathes slow, and soon his boy smell wraps us.

The night is old for him but not for me. I still have to look out, I still have to write our names in the water filmed on the windshield. By *our* I mean the grown man and myself who once slept one against and inside the other so easefully in this very seat and which is now so impossibly small we had to have been another branch of man to fit it.

This napping will do instead, this does. Of course the small wedge of boy is not the man's, but wedge it is, and I sleep until clouds come in their scene change and rain as loud as thunder wakes me or maybe it's the radio popping on because of wild electricity, or our shifting from its sudden start.

Lightning shows his little face mine. All its Xerox flicker lights my fear and fret, not in reflection but in duplication. I've made more of it, one wave after another, and I'm sorry. I try to warm him but he pulls in his breath like he doesn't need more than one, then he's awake.

Up and out is all there is to do—except for the rain sheeting the air loud and terrible and wet. The imprint of me to him gets stronger in two more flashes. It's my whole life tucked small in him, I see there will be no out.

This is the story of frogs, I say to calm him. How they fell from the sky in tiny droplets.

I don't like it, he says. Let me sleep.

That face again.

Listen, I say. Each frog is not the same the way all the snowflakes that fall are different.

It's not snowing, he yawns. It's cold though.

It rains thoroughly, it is a plague of rain. I don't know how I could see the stars at all before. B-B shot, I start again, but he's sleeping.

The car sticks to me nearly everywhere and the boy the rest. The car is a holster for what a boy always wants, the car is a form waiting for marzipan, then the car is a hideout filling with hope.

She learned her lesson and she laid in it is how I end the

story, listening hard, writing those names, watching them fog. But no listener likes stories with lessons because that means the listener didn't listen. Who likes to think, with ears always open, a listener can't listen?

Who likes to think?

I hug the boy to me, and it rains.

Water

WHAT ABOUT WATER?

Think hater, one different letter.

He's teetering on one leg because he doesn't want to sit in the sand but he doesn't want to stand on it either. Sand is too close, it's the first step to water. One leg is his best.

There's the water, in and out, up and down, I say. Seals like it a lot but they can't stand on one leg, can they?

I don't like seals, he says. He hops back to the towel, let's not forget the towel, its white-square-safe. Okay, okay, but don't let that foam creep up, he says as he sits on that towel with his toes just about touching shoved-up sand. No foam—and no birds.

The birds surround him, they put on long beaks and big

feet and walk right up to him. Let's eat, they squawk. My boy holds my knee.

We stay still until boredom remands the birds.

Sand—you play in it, I tell him. I kick it, I give it a forbidden kick while other mothers watch.

He sham-swims, belly to towel, he swims to the very edge with a lizardy whip of his bottom. I have some air left, he says, his cheeks wide with it.

Let's make angels in the sand, I say. Like snow. I flail my arms.

He catches a glistening stretch of plastic, like a jellyfish flattened, and he lets it grip and wind up his wrist. He's alive, he says.

I'm wiping sand off me all the way up my shoulder. You know better, I say.

Where's Dad? he says, like—I want him.

You remember, I say. At work. We are at play. So get some sticks, I say.

Sticks? He looks at me.

How else do you make a castle? You need sticks. I didn't bring a bucket.

He doesn't move from the towel. Where did he drown? he says.

Your uncle? I look away. Oh, like, between here and here.

With everyone watching? He covers his foot with sand. I wouldn't watch, he says.

It looked like swimming. He was on some kind of medicine so he just kept swimming. He swam too far. He didn't feel the cold of the water, I say. Where are those sticks?

He stretches from the towel edge to collect sticks. Is this stick good? Is this stick wood? He apprises the stickness of each, tries breaking one with the other, stirs the sand like a dish he's going to make me eat. When is Dad coming?

A vacation is not missing one person or the other, it's a man, a woman and a boy in one place together, especially when there's water. I say Soon. He's working but it's still a vacation, you know.

He doesn't.

The seals' nubs poke up way out there, looking like a man being swept off, a silhouette you can't quite see against a big slab of blue. Like a man you can't have, let alone save. I don't say Look, seals to this boy, I look down at my feet.

I made beer, he says, a cracked shell all beered up with foam at my feet.

I glug it down like a pirate, foam slides down my fingers.

You pretend, he says with a curl in his lip. He flat-foots the sand in his fury, he runs off, he runs his first run onto the sand without touching the sand, almost.

Why would a man swim so far who had too much to drink? He had the wrong sister. I am standing on the beach in my new small suit, waving and waving. And she is sitting, slouched over her baby, long before my baby.

We never go to the beach.

Get back here, I beg my boy. Not so close to the water. Not like that.

He prances now, he stretches his toes, he's almost touching. The horizon's up to his eye from behind, that big slab of blue that creeps.

I hold up a book but I can't row the words to block out that slab behind him, though nothing bad swims the blue of it, no killer whales or sharks—oh, probably sharks. I can't block the horizon because my son's in it, touching the blue foot of it, the way someone else did.

When I last ran the way he does next, the length of the water, dogs still ran behind. It was legal enough to let dogs run then, to bark at the foam and my sister and I and the man who had too much to drink, the man who drowned. My son returns himself with his drips and shakes off loose sand like any dog or that one from long ago, feet wet on the towel.

But it is progress, and the day is past halfway to dusk. The water now sucks toward us, then wrinkles in colors embarrassing to water: pink, orange, a gold only a fish could show. Who can't look at the ocean?

What's a buoy? my son asks.

Where girls aren't allowed, I say.

Boo-ee, he tells me, his lungs all tug.

Where did you hear such a word? I ask, as if even the

words of water are not to be mentioned, certainly not what's inside the waves, some relative.

See that, he says, some people said that's a buoy.

Something floats out there and of course everyone, myself included, remembers it from earlier, but now no one can.

It's a lost seal, says my son. We should throw it a fish.

A real lost seal? I say.

My son says Yes, it was on a vacation and it got in the ocean to work and got lost.

We watch it grow arms. People sit up.

It's him, I'll bet, swimming back from the dead, but I don't say that, I turn away in case he falters or disappears or turns out to be two birds flying low.

My sister turned away. The baby was crying.

Watch! My son pulls at me. Others murmur, there rises from them a shushing like an ocean, only without elegance, urgent, up on your feet.

The figure is now that much bigger that you can tell its sex—powerful arms, that kind of head. He's slow in his stroke, he must be tired says someone at my side. Then he's out and here and there, and without meaning to, people clap and he bows, water sluicing off the curl of his arm.

My son's hot on the sand, jumping from foot to foot, close to me. Where'd he come from? he asks as the man walks away.

A boat we can't see, says my husband, who has seen it all, walking down the bank from the lot.

I'll tell my sister, I say away from my son.

Quiet, says my husband, who can't know, with his hand on my arm and a kiss to my mouth, his face still at his work, lost to us still, even to my son who swarms the sand, legs and arms, who writhes in it in the ecstasy of a father's arrival.

What Did You Bring Me?

MONEY OR DEATH?

Go on, says my ex. He slides himself into a corner booth, tips one of the self-fluttering ferns on the mantle. Order something else.

No, I mean really—which sandwich, the one that costs so much with nothing in it or the one that will kill you with pastrami?

I should open a restaurant, he says. I could put food into it.

An old man in these shoes walks up with a pen. What'll it be?

Money or death? I ask him. Come on.

I love his sneakers, my ex says. I'll take the ham.

The same, I say.

In front of us sits a bowl of dip like entrails in a cup. Shoes like that on an old man is an optimistic sign, my ex says, dipping a chip in.

Optimistic? I say. Painted-on constellations shine overhead, but the stripe that bisects a continent in a corner is not latitude but water. This place?

From outside what the thug who enters brings in is all rain. I watch him take a seat at the card table with the toaster oven on top, put his feet up. But he doesn't loll back and look for stars like anyone would, like we are. Merry Christmas, he says, seeing me looking.

What do you want? is what I nearly say because he has that wanting look. I nod into my chips so it looks like I can hear his Merry but I'm too hungry to talk.

My ex cranes.

The thug hums behind a menu.

No greasy reindeer here, I observe. No shatterproof balls. All these no decorations signify a lack of hope on the part of the old man, I say.

The old man comes out with water. He says, Behind me, when I ask for the ladies where I duck to think about my ex, how he should open a restaurant and be done with it.

I have no money for that, my ex says when I return to bite into my ham. No music overhead or clang of the continents in the kitchen echo so the old man looks sharp at my ham as I bite into what the old man thinks there is no money for.

Why not open your front room or the garage and put in neon? To your success, I say, with some water.

The old man attends to the thug. What'll it be? to the thug sounds like Hegel. The thug orders what amounts to nothing and the man writes it down and goes off.

The thug leans on his elbows and asks in a soft voice: Your money or your life? Or is it, Your honey or your wife?

I blush and don't know what to do with my hands and my ex backs away from the table and starts to say, Hey! which changes to, Oh! when the old man comes out again with a gun.

That's not it, says the thug, turning it sideways. Wrong make.

Go on, says the old man. He walks over and bolts the door, turning it shut with a key.

Wait a minute, I say.

We wait.

The thug returns the gun to the old man who tucks it into his belt and leaves with the thug through the back. But not before they take our credit cards.

I guess the restaurant is ours, I say.

My ex complains about his luck.

We peer behind the door the old man and thug left by. Two girls lie in bonds between counters there, bound with strips from the tablecloth that must have covered the card table. They're not talking, they're bleeding.

Try the windows, I say. Since water's streaming over the butt of Antarctica, I'm sure the windows aren't sealed.

They are.

911 wants an address. We're locked in, I say, can't see a damn thing. Wait, the menu has a take-out number.

How can I know this isn't a crank call? sighs 911. No, says 911 to someone else, they don't deliver.

The girls cry, they accuse the thug of thuggery. Out of some corner my ex shakes his head then leans over the girls to untie their knots under their breasts which they are biting and then him.

We go sit under the ratio of miles to inches, waiting for cops, for one of us to break a window and leave. But we don't want to incur damages from the restaurant owner, wherever he is, so we don't. The girls bang at the kitchen door we have locked, bang like birds bent on breaking their necks.

I take it back about the restaurant business, says my ex. I'm comfortable already, he says.

I used to think you'd buy anything, I say.

We stare at the world. When I close my eyes to sleep, the cops being slow, I see rain and new sneakers, ones that old men would wear to run away in, that kids do after they ask, What did you bring me?

Lost the Baby

WHICH SITTER HAS HIM? We dropped him off so long ago, and we called so many. Suzie, I say, cupping my hand around the phone so the party is quieter, but Suzie's sitting triplets tonight, no sign of ours, and she makes the titter you get with triplets. I was just hoping, I say, with my own small laugh. The fourth sitter I call hangs up and I don't want that to happen again, I can't let it.

I might have to leave him again.

We were to pick him up at this prearranged time somewhere other than her place, that I remember. Like a drop, we'd joked, handing him over, as if he were an attaché case you'd plant under the raised gilt hoof of a statue or inside a culvert. At midnight I remember, because by then we'd have routed the drunkest and loudest and loneliest away from the dead soldiers and the little liquor's empties sinkside, but other partiers kept showing up with more drink and their talk, including men who held their gnarled desires in front of them like something homemade they couldn't return.

The clock in the kitchen says eight now, which it cannot be, given the dark night out the window and the hours long gone in greeting and in me asking Rachel's husband, Did he ever try breastmilk in pancakes? Rachel has already left but not her husband, who stands in front of Evelyn in the baby pool, stripped down to her tie-dye bra and panties. It is past midnight is what her outfit is saying, those ragged concentrics pointed at that husband who is dancing in the water to the big band with his shoes on in the water.

I don't go back to the kitchen. Frederick's in the way and his wrist bears a watch hidden in hairy tufts that if I could just bend a little backwards—but Leola's dress front has Frederick sidling into view and just as I'm angling myself watchwise, with all due consideration to the view and Leola, he unclasps that watch and slips it down her front.

Leola screams as if he has put his hand on her, which he does do after, on her elbow the way you are supposed to with screaming high-heeled women, but just then she hits him over the head with one of those shrunken party bags that hold Kleenex, keys, and, in her case, ketchup, a small pouch of which flies out and explodes with her half-meant blow.

So there he is, ostensibly bleeding, and I find ice, which

just makes him look like a brunch drink—someone has given him celery and he gets up to dance with it in his mouth as if it were a rose, sweeping Leola, all her apologetic length and front, under one arm, keeping the other outstretched, the stalk foremost, and his leg takes a stride that lands on the watch, which has slithered through whatever underwear and out.

The time? I say to the assembled.

What? is what they all answer.

The people behind me start yelling that the neighbors are pitching down wadded up newspaper, some of which they haven't read yet, the Sunday *Times* already, but shouldn't they throw something back? With people like that behind me and people like that in front of me, I can't turn around to see what happened to my husband because someone—could it be Eric?—is trying to kiss me.

Sweetheart! I shout as if I mean him. Perfect, I say, swiveling my breasts against his chest, then backing away.

My husband is pouring gin into the ear of someone he once worked with and therefore might again, someone who must have an ache there, who thinks a little soak might help but who is shrieking at the iciness of the tonic or at the bubbles anyway by the time I get over there to ask my husband about the time, and the baby, and the sitter's number.

But before he can say, What? like the others, people begin jumping with the big band rhythm, pogo-style, rave style, and then we are all jumping and still jumping when the cops come and my husband has to sweet talk them. In the ensuing sudden quiet, party members come forward with their coats on and take the stairs until it's just us and the cops, who finish off all the dip that nobody was having anyway, someone early on having dribbled scotch over the top. But these cops, they love the dip, the way they love Rachel's husband who tries to exit with Evelyn, the two of them both in her fur coat.

The number? I hiss to my own smiling husband. He's busy breaking out bubbly to wash down the dip, he says, Hush. Sure there's drugs being flushed or pushed, the cops tap their nails on their holsters in their what-have-we-here staccato.

My wife, says my husband, is drunk.

I roll my eyes at him, the mime's last resort, and the cops catch the domestic snap and laugh.

See you soon, we say to them as if they were guests, while they pick their way out, licking their lips. But as soon as the door closes, I shriek, the baby!

My husband has the number right here, but it is not right here or anywhere else for a long time, a long time of picking up newspaper balls and pieces of outfits and me starting to cry, and then he calls it and a machine voice answers, is happy to take a message but doesn't say for whom.

It is after three A.M., he says, and of course he is right, we are three hours late in picking up the baby.

I listen to our own machine play. Where are we? repeats in a low voice, more than twice, but the voice doesn't say Who with the Where.

A low voice, a low voice, says my husband. The one with no buzzer? The one you have to call from the street to get her to come to the door?

You don't stare at the door after the drop-off, thinking you'll need to know where again, especially when you're meeting elsewhere, especially when you're not coming back. My husband, not to mention me, is not yet quite sober, but he calls the number again from the street while I pound on one door and then another. When no one answers either, we holler the baby's name like he's old enough to open a window, and then we holler her name, and then someone throws down a piece of plastic from an appliance.

I remember this sitter, I say, she loves children. She can't have them. It'll be days before she calls. We might as well get the police now.

He says, No. No one wants a baby all the time. You'll see.

I will sleep on the street, I say.

My turtledove, he says, taking my arm. Yonder dawn.

The sun eases along the avenue like something sprung.

We go home, we lie down, and I dream that the baby says—as if he could talk, all grown up, unforgiving—I forgot you.

White

I'M AN OLD MAN BUT THAT is relative. That is, by having relatives you get old, by having children the old flag is up. Not skull and crossbones, not dead, though. You can be old without dead. Like this wood here with the sky coming through the joints. Here just some paint will make it old without dead. But only some colors. You think wood is good in any color but not old wood. Maybe black you think, no corners, no joints, no see-ums. No.

He sprays white across the barn.

Try white as the bag of flour you shake your chicken parts into. Arthritic chicken arms and legs.

He smiles.

A chicken's like a family: head, heart, wings. They get shook up in that bag of flour, they go off.

The boy's not listening. He is two parts boredom, two parts fear of getting white. The spray is as strong as the man's voice, only it goes everywhere. The boy wants that everywhere: white bush, white road, white hands—just not on him. Even on a chicken would be good, if there was one for this old barn, but no, it is not that old. There's just a cat for this barn, a cat who gets the white spray, and she ducks back into the barn quick, to kittens no doubt white too.

Your mother, he says, now she's not old, except to you, but she makes me old. She makes me real old.

His head and hat are now all white and the barn side is almost. Do you know what she said? You don't know. When you get old enough, you'll know. You'll wonder where all those chicken parts went.

The boy won't say what he knows. He cuffs the cat who comes out again. Is it thinking, Milk everywhere, fresh tits, moms all over the place? He heard his mother say she didn't have a mother, he heard it, her talking on the phone with her sister. Not that he listens usually, but the sound of that carried, like a tune out of tune. How could a mother not be one?

He turns that over. He believes they're signed on, mothers, you can't sign yourself off. Except for that boy who found a dead man in his bathroom, his mom.

Turn off the spigot, he says. Get my other hose. We'll finish up with the joints. That's where the age shows. Something butts up against something long enough you start seeing holes.

The boy drags the hose up.

Wrong end. The man wobbles his head No. Then he couples.

The dead man wasn't in the room a long time. It was just that if the boy had had a mom who stayed and been mom, she would have gone in there, to get a tissue, which is what they do. And if one mom can do that, not stay, then it can be done. And what about his? Her mom says no, I won't be mom, the rest will follow?

The paint follows, a thick trickle coming at his feet. Get that bucket, will you? he says.

White dirt, white torn-up shoes, white bent wire.

He puts out his hand as if to touch it, that not-at-all white hand so beige and pink and blue-veined, bright with a scar where he'd tried to poke in a design that would stay. The hand is not white at all.

You are your mother's boy. The man stomps the lid shut. You are just looking at it as it runs toward you, aren't you? Just looking at it.

The boy looks at it and away. The white comes for him but still he does nothing.

Damn, he says, having shoved the spray nozzle too close

to the joints so a part flies in, into a joint not bird- but bug-big. Now you go and get it.

The barn inside is what you can't guess from outside. First, a smell breaks from the paint in heaves: manure or hay that holds a sourness, or just a person's pee. And leather. Just belt and buckle leather because there is no horse skin there for any saddle, just a lot of old dish parts, and not the ones you eat off of but one of the ones with ears for electricity on steel webs that take in all those programs.

Behind the biggest part he finds the piece which has fallen. But by then the paint is coming through the joints all around in stripes like light and he is on his knees, his hand black in the dark so far away from his body that searching is like a bug running for cover when the paint finds him.

The man from outside sees only one more dark to make white.

The boy moves his hand. The turp is outside, beside the man who is mostly white and who will use most of it himself, later.

He hands him the piece he found with his striped white hand.

You have your mother's nose, he says.

The boy almost touches his nose, wants to touch it with his white hand. At least he has something of his mother, something she can't not be. The boy with the dead man in his bathroom, that boy, touched his own hand instead of that man's. He told him about touching his hand because he didn't want to touch the man's. He didn't have a mom.

You're a good boy, he says. But not for long, he says. Soon you'll be grown. And after grown comes what?

The boy chooses to move his feet, hide his hand.

Old, the man says. I'll never see you old. So you won't be.

He shuts off the spigot. The barn is all white. The man and the boy are almost as white as the barn.